This book is a treasure trove of informa
biblical challenges for all who work, whe
with children, in paid employment or
bring significance to the task. I cannot
this book who would not benefit from applying its wisdom.
Fiona Castle, Author, Speaker and Broadcaster

Here is a tonic for the workplace. *Working it Out* is biblical, practical and, above all, very readable. Ian Coffey's wisdom and honesty will inspire you as well as resource you.
Steve Chalke MBE, Founder – Oasis Global and Faithworks, UN.GIFT Special Advisor on Human Trafficking

Ian Coffey is a gifted and talented writer and this book will not disappoint. It will make you think and search your heart. It will inspire and enrich you.
Rosemary Conley CBE

Finding purpose at work is one of the greatest challenges for people today. In this very helpful book, it is wonderful to hear a pastor's view on how this can be achieved.
Ken Costa, Chairman of Lazard International and Alpha International, and Author of God at Work

Eleanor Roosevelt said 'find a job you love and you won't have to work a day in your life'. Easy eh? This book says that only one in three Britons enjoy their job. So, two-thirds don't. *Working it Out* should help Christians find purpose in the role they are in currently. The chapters will give the reader focus in the various stages of his or her career. With a combination of questions, lessons from Bible characters, real-life modern tales and ideas to use, this book can help you get the work–life balance right. So, don't let work kill you – let this book help!
Mark Holt, Founder and Managing Partner, Mark Holt and Co.

I originally heard the content of much of this book in Ian Coffey's *God@work.com* sermon series some years ago and I am delighted that it is now available for all to read. As a motivational speaker I stand in front of thousands of business people every month. Ian's practical and action-provoking words challenged me to stop leaving my faith at the door on Monday mornings. To admit openly on stage to my audiences that I live my life for Christ was initially terrifying, but it has transformed the nature of my job and given my work-life new purpose. *Working it Out* demonstrates that all of us could and should be uttering those infamous *Chariots of Fire* words 'when I run I feel His pleasure' about our own jobs.
Debra Searle MBE, Professional Adventurer and Motivational Speaker

The 'it' I have been trying to work out for some time is what does God want me to do? Related questions include, 'Am I in the right place, or job?' or 'How do I give back?', often resulting in the 'Take the leap of faith, see what happens, God will provide' type of response. I imagine that further along the Christian journey, these issues become more perplexing. Writing as one who has started the journey relatively late, this is a milestone book, and one of the many 'aha' moments contained therein is that changing your perspective is more important than changing your situation. I don't mean half-full or half-empty glasses; I'm talking about enjoying the beer. I thank God for inspiring Ian to help me answer the question. It is hugely liberating not having to worry any more about the 'it'.
Nicolas Versloot, Strategic Planning Director, Birra Peroni

Until now I've only had one book I feel I can wholeheartedly recommend that all people in the workplace should buy – *Thank God it's Monday* by Mark Greene. At last there is another one I can encourage people to read alongside it. In *Working it Out*, Ian Coffey enables us to understand God's view on our work, empowers us to connect our faith to our daily working lives, and encourages us to make a difference for Christ in our workplaces.
Jago Wynne, Workplace Minister, All Souls, Langham Place, London

Ian Coffey

WORKING IT OUT

God, you and the work you do

ivp

Inter-Varsity Press
Norton Street, Nottingham NG7 3HR, England
Email: ivp@ivpbooks.com
Website: www.ivpbooks.com

British Library Cataloguing in Publication Data
A catalogue record for this book is available from the British Library.

ISBN 978–1–84474–219–6

Set in Dante 12/15
Typeset in Great Britain by CRB Associates, Reepham, Norfolk
Printed and bound in Great Britain by Ashford Colour Press Ltd, Gosport, Hampshire

Inter-Varsity Press publishes Christian books that are true to the Bible and that communicate the gospel, develop discipleship and strengthen the church for its mission in the world.

Inter-Varsity Press is closely linked with the Universities and Colleges Christian Fellowship, a student movement connecting Christian Unions in universities and colleges throughout Great Britain, and a member movement of the International Fellowship of Evangelical Students. Website: www.uccf.org.uk

For Alan Johnson

In appreciation of a friend and
colleague who consistently
takes his faith to work

CONTENTS

ACKNOWLEDGMENTS

Thank-yous are really important, not simply for those who receive them (as we all like to be appreciated), but also for those offering the thanks. We are reminded that none of us are soloists, but team players.

A team of people has been responsible for this book, even though it has my name on the cover. This is my opportunity to acknowledge their inspiration, encouragement, ideas, patience and goodwill.

Mark Greene set me off on a journey I describe in these chapters and for which I am most grateful. Mark is someone I enjoy knowing because he always makes me think even when I don't want to. He is a gift to the church of Christ.

Kate Byrom and the team at IVP are great publishers and make writing books an enjoyable part of my life.

Martin and Jill Kingston kindly allowed me to use Les Fonteneilles as a quiet haven where much of this book was written. No writer could fail to be inspired by such magnificent surroundings, and I am one of many to benefit from Martin's and Jill's generosity and willingness to share their home.

This book is dedicated to my friend Alan Johnson, who has served as CEO of Spring Harvest since 1990. His integrity and desire to live out his faith at work are an eloquent testimony. I have spent a number of years working alongside Alan and his staff at Spring Harvest. To describe that as a privilege is an understatement. The pursuit of excellence and warm team spirit of the Spring Harvest staff is quite remarkable. They are special people to work with and, in their own way, have (unknowingly) contributed to this book.

Ruth is my life partner and closest friend who reads everything I write. Her comments and insights have made important contributions along the way and her experience of the world of work has helped to earth the material in these chapters.

Nigel Majikari has been my prayer partner through what has been for both of us a turbulent time in our respective worlds of work. We have puzzled and prayed our way through it together and there are marks of that journey on these pages.

I am indebted to various writers who have written on this topic and where possible I have mentioned the relevant books. But, as a busy pastor, I have not always noted down the source of a quote or illustration and apologize in advance for any omissions.

Finally, to those members of my congregations in Plymouth, England and Ferney Voltaire, France – thank you for your insights and examples that have helped me understand more about discipleship in the workplace. Added to these is a long list of people who have shared their stories and helped me understand more clearly what God is up to when he is not in church.

Ian Coffey
Geneva
January 2008

SERIES PREFACE

A time for courage

Work matters hugely.

Work is the primary activity God created us to pursue – in communion with him and in partnership with others. Indeed, one of work's main goals is to make God's world a better place for all God's creatures to flourish in – to his glory.

Yes, work matters hugely.

And to many people it brings the joys of purpose shared, relationships deepened, talents honed, character shaped, obstacles overcome, products made, people served and money earned – even amid the inevitable frustrations, failures and disagreements of working life in even the best of organizations.

Yes, work matters hugely. And so it matters hugely that for many people, most people actually, work is not only getting harder, longer, less satisfying and more draining, but is stretching its voracious tentacles into almost every area of life, sucking out the zing and whoosh and ease from time with family, friends, hobbies and community activities. UK citizens, for example, work four hours longer per person per week than the citizens of any other EU nation. We live in Slave New World.

How do we follow Jesus faithfully and fruitfully in such conditions?

Is coping – getting through the week – the height of our ambition? Surely not. But do we have good news for the workplace? Not just a truth to proclaim but a way to follow. Not just a way to follow but life, divine life, to infuse the quality of our work, the quality of our relationships at work, and the quality of our contribution to the culture of the organizations in which we work? In our current context, we need not only biblical insight and divine empowerment, but also courage to make tough decisions *about* work and life, and courage to make tough decisions *at* work.

That's what the Faith and Work series is designed to do: take on the tough issues facing workers and offer material that's fresh, either because it brings new insights to familiar topics or because the author's particular background and experience open up enlightening vistas. We've also tried to write the books so that there's something nutritious and tasty, not only for the leisurely diner, but also for the snacker snatching a quick read on a train, or in a break, or, indeed, at the end of a demanding day.

The Lord be with you as you read. And the Lord be with you as you seek to follow him faithfully and courageously in your workplace.

Mark Greene
Series Editor
London Institute for Contemporary Christianity
2008

Volumes include:
Get a Life Paul Valler
Working Models for our Time Mark Greene (commissioned)
Working Without Wilting Jago Wynne (commissioned)

BIG EARS

Ian Coffey has big ears.

Not physically, but metaphorically. You expect pastors to have big hearts and he has one of those too. But it's the combination that's so formidable. Ian listens. Yes, Ian knows what it's like to get up early of a morning, commute an hour and a half each way and work in a law firm – but, more importantly, he has listened to people who do a whole host of different jobs. He's a pastor who has genuinely grasped just how significant work, paid or unpaid, is in people's lives, just how deep the challenges are to living out a vibrant faith in today's workplace and just how vital it is that we do – for our own sake, for the compelling model it is to others, and for the fruitfulness of our ministry and witness in those contexts.

Ian has taken all that to heart for years now in his own churches: facilitating meetings of people in similar jobs, opening himself up to detailed questionnaire feedback on his preaching and teaching, asking people what topics they need input on, and soliciting prayer requests about people's daily occupations. And that's just what I know about.

Ian's on the side of the workers. He doesn't believe that the job of the pastor is to create a bigger church with lots of programmes, but to help people grow in their walk and fruitfulness for Christ in the places and among the people he's called them to love and serve. And because Ian's for the workers, and knows we're busy, strained and stressed, he won't let us get away with saying that we don't have time to devote to growing in Christ. Oh yes, he knows we may not have time to be on a committee or a rota, but he also knows that if we're not listening to the word, praying with others, accountable to someone and encouraged by fellowship, our adventure with Christ may wither faster than Jonah's gourd. Most of the books on work have been written by people who've spent a fair amount of time in the secular workplace. I'm one of them, and there's quite a number out there now. But Ian is offering us a different angle, a pastor's angle, the angle of someone who has opened his big ears to people and who yearns not only that we would work well in Christ, but also that we would live our whole life well in Christ.

This book also reflects Ian's journey. Not every pastor has a vision for how God can work through work, and Ian hasn't always had that either. He has worked it out. So this book is an encouragement to us all, to pastors and people, that church communities can change and be used to envision and support the workers to make a difference in their workplace to the glory of God.

May it be so.

Mark Greene
Series Editor
London Institute for Contemporary Christianity
2008

INTRODUCTION: MY JOURNEY TO WORK

I was once on a plane journey with a man who told me that his wife was a Christian but, although he went to church with her most weeks, he didn't share her faith – at least not yet.

I asked him what he thought when he attended church on a Sunday. He looked at me quizzically. 'You really want to know?' he asked. I told him I did. I have never forgotten his answer: 'I often sit in church after a hard week at work handling all kinds of pressures and I sit there thinking, "This is completely irrelevant to my life. You simply haven't got a clue about living in my world."'

Ouch.

> 'I sit in church after a hard week at work and I think, "This is completely irrelevant to my life."'

Mark Greene has a 'Monday at 11.00' test. If what people are learning in church on Sunday at 11.00 has little relevance to where they are and what they are doing on Monday at 11.00, then something is seriously wrong.

That was certainly the case with the man I sat next to on the plane.

Mark Greene is the Director of the London Institute for Contemporary Christianity (and Series Editor for this book). He once asked me if I had ever preached on the theology of work. I fluffed around the answer. But he was persistent: he was conducting a research project on the subject. Eventually, he got me thinking.

One day, sitting in my study and trying to plan the next term's teaching programme, I began some mental doodling.

What did 'workplace theology' look like? Yes, there were books on the Christian and the workplace, on ethics in business and on 24/7 discipleship. They could give me some clues. But simply to read some books and reproduce the writers' ideas in sermon form would be cheating. Instead I decided to do what I think is always best when it comes to preaching: start with the Bible and work outwards.

That is when I discovered how much the Bible has to say on the topic of work. To say it was a revelation sounds cheesy. So let's call it a discovery, or, if you are really spiritual, an epiphany.

I was blown away by how much the best book in the world has to say about work, whether it is paid or unpaid. I got really excited. Not that it was surprising to find Scripture so relevant to this area of our lives, but I had never addressed the question of work so specifically. I wished I could have brought some of what I discovered to my conversation with the man on the plane.

> **I was blown away by how much the best book in the world has to say about work.**

After some reading and note-taking, I found I had so much material that it would be a case of what to leave out. The Bible is packed with wisdom on this subject.

My research resulted in a sermon series entitled 'God@work.com', which ran for three months or so. At that point in my ministry, we were based in a city-centre church in Plymouth, which had a large and varied congregation. Running parallel to the series we arranged a prayer initiative, which is outlined later in the book. Following the teaching programme, we also arranged several breakfasts drawing together people in different lines of work with the purpose of providing a forum for meeting and sharing.

As a pastor and preacher, I was encouraged by the feedback I received as members of the church family spoke openly about coming to a new place in relating their faith to their job. I was particularly encouraged by those in the congregation who were not in paid employment, but led busy lives caring for small children or sick relatives. Some spoke of finding a sense of meaning in a role that at times felt meaningless.

I then received a call to an international church in France, very close to the city of Geneva. It was a congregation drawn from up to fifty nations, and many members were expatriates working on short-term contracts before moving to a posting elsewhere. Our turnover of people was enormous and that created some peculiar pressures as well as some unique opportunities. I had to adapt my teaching on workplace theology in the light of the particular issues, outlined below, that were faced by my new congregation.

- Adapting to a multicultural approach to work where colleagues from other countries held different values.
- The insecurity produced by short-term contracts.
- The upheaval of moving every few years to a new country.
- The constant 'where do I really belong?' feeling.
- Family issues where children were born in one culture, grew up in one or more new cultures, and then adapted to what has been called the 'third culture' unique to international children.
- The struggle of trying to build relationships with people who move on.
- The stress of being away from family – especially when facing some of life's big moments.

I came to understand that this world of work looked quite different from the one in the UK and I needed to adapt my teaching and pastoring accordingly.

One of our interns during our time in Geneva was an Italian student named Ester. She had a fruitful ministry among teenagers and her language skills made her an instant hit in our multilingual community.

Out of the blue, Ester was invited to a high-school graduation at an exclusive Swiss school. Much to her excitement (and others' too), the principal announced a surprise visit from an honoured guest. Michael Douglas took the podium to enthusiastic applause. Perhaps, for once, graduation day was going to prove more fun than watching paint dry.

The immaculately groomed star began by thanking his host and congratulating the graduating students. He then announced the theme of his sermon – sorry, speech. 'I want to talk today', he began, 'about the difference between success and significance.'

He reminded the students that their privileged backgrounds had provided them with an excellent education in comfortable surroundings. With all this behind them and a willingness to work hard, they would not struggle to find success along whichever path they chose to tread. But there is an ocean of difference between success and significance. He spent some minutes spelling out what each of the two destinations looked like, before leaving his audience with a question that hung in the air: 'Do you want to live a successful life, or a significant one?'

My friend Ester came away deeply affected by what Michael Douglas had shared. She felt she had heard the gentle voice of Jesus speaking to her. She was facing some important choices concerning her own future and, in a most unexpected way, she had heard from God.

This book is about discovering significance, particularly in the world of work. It is for people who are following Jesus and want to integrate their faith and work life. Whether you are a high-flying entrepreneur or a mum with three pre-schoolers screaming for your attention, I think there are things in this book that will be relevant.

It is also for people like me who teach the Bible, lead churches and do their level best to offer help and support to those who struggle at times with some of the things life throws up in their faces. I hope this book will spark your own imagination and open up some relevant passages of the Bible in new ways.

There's a joke that has been doing the rounds for some time. It starts with the question, 'Why don't Baptist pastors look out of the window of their offices in the morning?' Answer: 'Because they'd have nothing to do all afternoon.'

I agree, it's unfair – but at least it's funny.

Any of us who are called to servant leadership in Christ's church know a good deal about the real world and about people's hopes and struggles. Some of us spent time in secular work before responding to God's call to serve. (I worked for a number of years in a busy law office and spent three hours a day commuting in and out of London.) The experience is there: what is sometimes missing is the ability to bridge the world of the Bible and the world where people live. That is a skill we all need to develop and refine.

This book is an offering of some of the biblical material on work together with insights gleaned from others who have written on the topic. Woven into this are many stories that come from the kind of real-life conversations pastors have with their congregation. As they say at the end of film credits, 'names have been changed to respect privacy' – but not all have been changed, for reasons that will become apparent.

My encounter on the plane showed me how people can sit in church feeling that it has no relevance to their real lives. Perhaps – by God's grace – they may find their way into the family of faith through some practical teaching on how faith and work go together.

It is my hope that reading this book will help you understand a little more about how following Jesus involves every part of life, especially work.

I recently visited a member of my congregation who had undergone major surgery. A few weeks before, he was made redundant by the company that had moved him from the UK to Geneva a few years previously. We talked about how we can make sense of such events and trust God to work them out for our good. My visit was coming to a close and we agreed to pray together. I pulled out a small New Testament in *The Message* paraphrase and read these words from Romans:

> **Every part of life – even the sad bits – can be lived to the glory of God.**

> So here's what I want you to do, God helping you: Take your everyday, ordinary life – your sleeping, eating, going-to-work, and walking-around life – and place it before God as an offering.[1]

We concluded that this covered unexpected redundancy as well. Every part of life – even the sad bits – can be lived to the glory of God.

Martin Luther King, the Baptist preacher and civil rights activist, was once invited to speak to a group of junior high school students. He left his young audience with some life-shaping advice they would never forget: 'If it falls to your lot to be a street sweeper, sweep streets like Michelangelo painted pictures, sweep streets like Beethoven composed music, sweep streets like Shakespeare wrote poetry. Sweep streets so well that all the hosts of heaven and earth will have to pause and say: Here lived a great street sweeper who swept his job well.' Six months later, King was cut down by an assassin's bullet outside a Memphis motel, but his legacy lingers and his succinct counsel to young people on the brink of the world of work has no sell-by date.

I don't know if Michael Douglas knew about this speech before he made his own. But I believe he understood the wisdom that lay behind Martin Luther King's words.

You may be a busy mum, an influential business executive, a bricklayer, a nuclear scientist, an engineer, a postal worker or a street cleaner. Whoever you are and whatever you do, your work gives you a great opportunity to be significant.

For further thought . . .

1. Consider the hard-hitting comment of the man on the plane: 'I often sit in church after a hard week at work handling all kinds of pressures and I sit there thinking, "This is completely irrelevant to my life. You simply haven't got a clue about living in my world." ' How does your experience of church match up to this? How could church better equip you to live for God during the week? Could you speak to your minister, small-group leader or fellow members to discuss this?

2. Success or significance. Do you know of anyone who has been significant without being obviously successful? Or successful without being significant? What can we avoid or follow from their example?

3. In what ways do you currently find it easy or difficult to live out your faith at work?

1. CURSE OR BLESSING?

In the Walt Disney classic film *Snow White and the Seven Dwarfs*, there is an instantly recognized and catchy little tune, 'Hi ho, hi ho, it's off to work we go'. The movie was made at the end of the Great Depression of the 1930s and is an interesting reflection of that period. It was a time when millions did not have paid work and lacked a sense of personal value. No matter how mundane your job, the fact of having one and being able to put bread on the table might well have made you want to whistle while you worked!

But things are different today. You may have seen the bumper sticker that parodies the seven dwarfs' song: 'I owe, I owe, it's off to work we go'. For many, work is simply a means of paying the mortgage and the bills. There is no sense of fulfilment or purpose beyond the daily grind. Some find work simply a chore and, given the freedom to choose, would look for a more fulfilling job.

Which is closest to your view of the world of work: the original song, or the bumper sticker? Is it a privilege or a chore, a curse or a blessing?

Tony is a car mechanic and his wife, Jo, is a practice nurse in a GP's surgery. They met as teenagers at their local church youth club, which Tony now helps to run. Some months ago at their home group, the subject of work came up in

> **For many, work is simply a means of paying the mortgage and the bills.**

discussion. Rob, who leads the group, suggested some ways in which we can worship God through our work. Tony responded with a mixture of surprise and amusement. The last place you could worship God, in Tony's opinion, was his garage!

Tony did acknowledge that God wants us to help people in the course of our daily lives, because that is all about loving our neighbour. But he felt work was nothing more than a way of getting through life and having enough cash to support the family. In Tony's view, God didn't create us to work. It was a direct result of human rebellion.

Is it correct that work is a consequence of what is known as 'the fall'? If you ask those who are familiar with the Bible, 'What does God think about work?' they might point to the opening chapters of Genesis and God's words of judgment against Adam:

> Cursed is the ground because of you;
>> through painful toil you will eat of it
>> all the days of your life.
> It will produce thorns and thistles for you,
>> and you will eat the plants of the field.
> By the sweat of your brow
>> you will eat your food
> until you return to the ground,
>> since from it you were taken;
> for dust you are
>> and to dust you will return.[1]

Sin had consequences and Adam and Eve lost much as a result. The banishment from the Garden of Eden (symbolizing the loss of immortality) is described in these words:

> So the LORD God banished him from the Garden of Eden to work the ground from which he had been taken.[2]

Humankind fell into sin and missed God's best. Fellowship with God was broken, relationships were impaired – paradise was lost. Pain in childbirth and hard physical work were added to the mix of the sorry mess of human rebellion.

Such a reading of Scripture suggests that work is indeed a curse and a direct result of living in a fallen world. But that is a faulty interpretation, which doesn't take account of the whole of Genesis 1 – 3, nor indeed the rest of the Bible. It offers a wrong foundation on which to build an understanding of life.

> **Work is a blessing from the hand of God.**

If we read the whole of the Genesis story, we discover that work is a blessing from the hand of God. Even in a fallen world, work can become a window of grace.

To begin to understand this we need to look briefly at God's character, God's command and God's call.

God's character

Ask a group of friends, 'What do you find really fulfilling?' and you will probably get a rich mixture of replies. I have a friend who tells me that a day organizing her garden gives her an enormous buzz; another says it's cooking a delicious meal for a houseful; one (who really needs to get out more) is never happier than when surrounded by spreadsheets and columns of figures. I have a son who thinks being covered in mud and bruises at the end of a bone-crunching game of rugby on a wet winter's day is sheer heaven, and another who reckons that teaching a bunch of children to read is more fun than flying. But, for all our differences, most of us recognize that warm glow of fulfilment that exclaims, 'I really like that!'

That feeling is an echo of the truth that human beings are made in God's image. As the universe was shaped and fashioned, God delighted in his handiwork. The Big Bang had an author and its aftermath a sculptor as divine fingers shaped a universe of limitless wonders. Genesis records:

> **God is by nature creative – he is a workman.**

> God saw all that he had made, and it was very good.[3]

We are offered the image of an artist working intensely on a canvas then standing back to take in the masterpiece with a feeling of immense satisfaction and achievement. God is by nature creative – he is a workman.

A family likeness

It is sometimes easy to spot people from the same family, not simply because they look alike, but because they carry something else that links them – a mannerism, a gesture, or a facial expression. The Genesis account teaches that we are made in the image of God, after his likeness:

> Then God said, 'Let us make human beings in our image, in our likeness, and let them rule over the fish of the sea and the birds of the air, over the livestock, over all the earth, and over all the creatures that move along the ground.'

> So God created human beings
>   in his own image,
>   in the image of God
>   he created them;
>   male and female
>   he created them.[4]

As well as sharing something of God's likeness, we are called to rule and reign – and work – within the creation that he has made.

This is both a high and a holy calling that should humble and amaze us. As King David wrote in one of his prayer songs:

> What are mere mortals that you are mindful of them,
>   human beings that you care for them?
> You made them a little lower than the heavenly beings
>   and crowned them with glory and honour.
> You made them rulers over the works of your hands;
>   you put everything under their feet.[5]

In all the ongoing debates about our world and its resources, the threats to the environment, the depletion of the ozone layer, the protection of species of animals, birds and fish, the exploration of space and oceans, and genetic research, the Bible sends a vital signal.

It is God's world before it is our world. We are entrusted with the responsibility of being stewards of those things he has committed to our care. A steward is a guardian – someone looking after something that belongs to another. When we view the universe through that filter, everything takes on a different colour.

We hear much of human rights and that is an important matter, especially in those parts of the global community where people still live in fear under the rule of tyrants. But on the other side of the same coin lie what we could describe as human responsibilities. First and foremost they are to God, and secondly to our neighbour, as summed up in the two great commandments according to Jesus.[6]

We have a privileged position at the apex of God's creation and it carries responsibilities. Emphasizing privilege at the expense of responsibility produces a lopsided view of life.

> **Privilege without responsibility produces a lopsided view of life.**

We can trace the God image in a number of ways and one of them is the capacity to create, work and find fulfilment in such things. Ulrich Zwingli (1484–1531) was a leader in the great Reformation of the church that swept across Europe in the sixteenth century and stood alongside men such as Martin Luther and John Calvin. Zwingli wrote:

There is nothing in the universe so like God as the worker.

He was acknowledging that when we see a man or a woman going about their work, we catch a glimpse of the character and the nature of the God who made them.

Or take an example from the award-winning film *Chariots of Fire*. It tells the story of Eric Liddell, a man who had a call from God to be a missionary and who also had an amazing athletic ability. His sister was really worried that he was missing God's best, and so she challenged him that his love of athletics was eclipsing his devotion to Christ. Eric responded with a burning passion: 'I believe God made me for a purpose – for China. But he also made me fast and when I run, I feel his pleasure.'

Are there particular tasks or activities in your life that make you feel good? Is it adding up a row of figures and making them balance? Is it making a cake? Is it caring for an elderly relative, or teaching a child to tie her shoelaces? Is it winning a contract? Is it seeing a class change over the course of two or three terms? Is it mowing a lawn, or making a chair, or repairing a car, or helping someone die with dignity? Thank God for helping you to spot the family likeness.

Take the story of Leonardo da Vinci, who had almost completed a painting on which he had been working for months. He was surrounded by a group of students watching the master craftsman at his work. As he reached the final touches, he handed a brush to one of his students and said, 'Finish it.'

The astonished young man protested, 'I haven't got the talent – I am not worthy.'

Da Vinci replied, 'Will not what I have done inspire you to do your best?'

As we consider the universe with wonder and worship and marvel at our Creator God, so we are inspired to display the family likeness through our work.

Key point
God in his nature is a worker. We are made in his image – and our capacity to work and discover fulfilment displays the family likeness.

God's command

The Genesis story reveals two basic instructions that God gave to men and women, which we can summarize in this way:

- Be fruitful.[7]
- Be useful.[8]

The first is the command to fill the earth, to procreate and exercise authority over all created things. The second is to work the land and take care of it. Adam was not given a deckchair and a parasol, but a shovel and a rake – and this was before the fatal act of rebellion against God's rule and its awful consequences. So work was commanded *before* the fall took place; it was a command from God and as such should be seen as an expression of the privileged position of stewardship Adam was called to undertake.

> **Adam was not given a deckchair and a parasol, but a shovel and a rake.**

As God gives Adam his new responsibility, he recognizes that he lacks a partner and so the Genesis story reveals the creation of Eve, 'a helper suitable for him'.[9] A richer way of translating that is 'a helper matching him and supplying what he lacks'. Men and women share God's gifts and responsibilities as partners and co-stewards.

The decisions made – first by Eve and then by Adam – to turn their backs on God led to banishment from the beautiful garden made for them to work in and enjoy. Pride (which lies at the root of all sin) led to separation from God, loss of privilege, loss of innocence, loss of immortality and the introduction of sickness and disease. Eve was told that childbirth would become more painful and Adam that work would become more wearisome. Everything was affected by the choice to rebel – even the world of work was damaged.

But we should not buy into the mistaken idea that work did not exist before the great separation. Before the fall God gave work as a creation gift. It is a living definition of what it means to be human.

Key point
Work is a creation gift from God. When we work we express our privileged role as stewards of God's creation.

God's call

I am so glad that the Bible doesn't stop at Genesis, but goes through the other sixty-five books to spell out a wonderful story of grace, forgiveness and a God who didn't abandon his fallen and flawed creation.

How lost people can be found sums up the theme of the Bible, and the central character in the story is the Lord Jesus Christ, God's Son.

Jesus is described as the second Adam – who came to put right the mess made by the first one.[10] The pages of the Old Testament point to his coming and the pages of the New Testament explain how it happened and all that has become possible as a result.

The great themes of salvation (being made whole), redemption (being bought out of slavery), justification (being declared not guilty), atonement (sin being covered and wiped away), sanctification (how by God's power we can live holy lives) and glorification (the wonderful hope that we will be with Christ for ever, made complete in him) are all traced to what Jesus has accomplished by his death on the cross and resurrection. Such themes have inspired paintings and music, architecture and literature for centuries. In Christ alone we can find forgiveness and peace with God. The gospel (or good news) offers hope to people who are lost.

How, then, does the gospel of Christ touch my world of work? It has a lot to do with being called to follow Christ.

In the first place, we need to recover the forgotten years. Jesus was crucified at thirty-three years of age after a public ministry that lasted for three years. For thirty years he lived in relative obscurity in an unglamorous and small community in the region of Galilee. He worked in a carpenter's shop following the family trade. It would appear that Joseph –

Mary's husband – died when Jesus was young and he took responsibility as eldest son for the others in his family.

Jesus knew how to work with wood and make a door frame. His customers were farmers and tradesmen and some probably didn't pay their bills. He knew how to work until the sweat poured down, he hit his thumb with a hammer, he knew what aching tiredness felt like and he understood the glow of satisfaction at a job well done.

> **Jesus understood the glow of satisfaction at a job well done.**

Jesus lived an ordinary life.

Joy has cared for her son, David, for the last twenty-seven years. David has cerebral palsy and, in recent years, other health difficulties. Joy's husband left them both many years ago and ever since she has cared for David as a single parent. Joy's life revolves around meeting her David's needs night and day. She has help in various forms, but she is the main carer and the one who carries the responsibility for David. Joy takes great inspiration from the example of Jesus and the forgotten years in Nazareth. When anyone praises her devotion, Joy brushes the compliment aside, not because it is unappreciated, but because she sees what she does as a calling rather than a burden. She admits to getting tired and wonders if her own health will stand up to the increasing demands. But when asked for the source of her inspiration, she points to Jesus – and not in some twee way, because hers is a rugged get-out-of-bed-in-the-early-hours kind of faith.

William Barclay's prayer reminds us about the way Jesus touched ordinariness and made it special:

O God our Father
We remember how the eternal word became flesh and dwelt
    among us.

We thank you that Jesus did a day's work like any working
man.

That he knew the problem of living together in a family.

That he knew the frustration and irritation of serving the
public.

That he had to earn a living and to face all the wearing
routine of everyday work and life and living.

And so clothe each common task with glory.[11]

It is said that Billy Graham and his late wife, Ruth, in their
home in Montreat in North Carolina, had a plaque over
the kitchen sink which said, 'Divine service conducted here
three times daily.' That is a tremendous statement of what
Jesus does. He touches the ordinary
and makes it special. You can do
the dishes, weld a gatepost, or
dress a shop window to the glory
of God.

**You can weld
a gatepost
to the glory
of God.**

If we are not careful, we can run
away with the notion that if you are
a missionary or a vicar, then you must be very important in
terms of God's kingdom. If you are a politician or hold a
high-profile job, then angels must hold their breath when one
of your prayers arrives in heaven. But if your everyday work
doesn't hit the headlines or attract prayers in church services,
then it cannot be that high up the spiritual values scale. We
even have a way of acknowledging that. When we meet
someone and they ask what we do for a living, some of us
reply, 'I'm *just* a homemaker and mum,' or 'I *just* run
a shop.'

Take that little word *just* away and burn it! If you are a
disciple of Christ, that in itself is your job title and job description. Look no further for dignity or worth.

And by the way, don't forget the ordinariness of some of the key characters of the Bible.

Abraham was a travelling farmer and entrepreneur.

Moses lived part of his life in a royal palace where he was intellectually trained and part as a shepherd before God called him.

Joseph was big in animal husbandry, served as a household servant and spent a spell in prison as a 'trusty' before achieving high government office.

Ruth was a widow, a refugee, a farm labourer and a housewife.

Esther was a lady with supermodel looks who became a queen.

Daniel was a civil servant.

David was a shepherd, musician, soldier and king (not all at the same time!).

Amos was a shepherd and a farmer.

Isaiah served in a royal court.

Nehemiah was an expatriate who worked as a butler to the king.

Elisha was a wealthy landowner.

William Tyndale, the man who translated the New Testament into the English language, wrote these words:

> There is no better work than to please God. To pour water, to wash dishes, to be a cobbler or an apostle is all one. To wash dishes or to preach is all as one as touching the deed to please God.

Rightly, Tyndale is saying that our aim should be to serve God wherever he has put us and to give of our very best.

My friend Dave became a Christian in his mid-forties. He was a manager of a large company in our town and a popular member of the local cricket club. He and his wife, Jill, attended a discipleship group that my wife and I ran for new Christians. We were meant to be introducing the group to the basics of the Christian faith, but, as often happens, we received from the group more than we gave.

One of my memories of Dave was his determination to integrate his new-found faith with every part of life. The way he ran his business, dealt with his employees and even played cricket was all run through this new filter of being a follower of Jesus. To be frank, I struggled to keep up at times. His constant questioning every week sometimes threw me off course. But his persistence challenged me and was an inspiration to others in the group. You see, Dave wanted a faith that worked all the time and not just on Sundays.

Key point
Jesus calls us to follow him. Discipleship is worked out in the everyday world of work and relationships. Whatever my job, my work is important to God.

Imagine I visit you and ask you to show me your church. You may take me along the street to a large ornate building with big towers and stained-glass windows. Or it may be a modern building with a car park, or perhaps a small hut with a corrugated roof, or even a community hall you hire for the weekends. I am sure you would be geographically correct – after all, you know where your church meets better than I do – but theologically you'd be quite wrong.

If you want to show me your church, I need to visit the supermarket and meet the checkout girl, or go into the school and see the teacher of 4e at work. Then there's the man who drives heavy articulated lorries around the motorway network. There are the several mums caring for pre-schoolers and the people looking after elderly friends and family.

If I want to meet your church, the last place I'd look is in an empty building. Church is community, it's people, and they don't cease to be part of the living church of Christ when they walk through the doors of an office, school or supermarket on Monday morning at 8.30. If we grasp this truth, then the world of work takes on a whole different meaning. It is part of my call to follow Christ. My work – whether paid or unpaid – is not opposed to my discipleship, but is part of it.

George Herbert, the seventeenth-century poet, captured it perfectly when he wrote these wonderful words:

Teach me, my God and King,
In all things thee to see,
And what I do in anything
To do it as for thee.

When we look at life this way, everything takes on a new meaning. Whatever my world of work may look like, when I treat it as a blessing rather than a curse, it brings God into the picture. And, as always, he makes everything different.

For further thought . . .

1. What do you find really fulfilling? How does that warm glow of achievement help you to realize that you are made in the image of God?

2. If your daily work is a result of 'a creation command from God', how does this affect your attitude to your work?

3. 'Jesus lived an ordinary life.' How does this truth inspire you in your work and relationships?

2. WHAT DOES GOD DO ON MONDAYS?

When I was at theological college we had a custom every day of praying for former students. We used prayer cards people sent in that said things like 'Please pray for so-and-so working as a vicar in Manchester', or 'Please remember this couple working as medical missionaries in Thailand'. One morning a prayer card sent waves of stifled laughter around the college chapel. The prayer request was simply this: 'Please pray for Fred, who is currently serving Jesus in a Chinese restaurant in Peckham.'

After the suppressed laughter had passed, I realized the profound point. According to the apostle Paul, Fred was indeed serving Jesus, no matter who paid his wages.

When we look at the New Testament letters, we discover that God is interested in our work life as much as he is in our so-called Christian activities. Every part of life is to be lived as followers of Christ.

We can serve the Lord Jesus in a Chinese restaurant, or by digging a hole, hanging washing, changing a washer, preparing the papers for a board meeting, or fixing a dripping tap. If you are a child of God, Paul's crisp statement says it all:

It is the Lord Christ you are serving.[1]

But we don't always live as though this is true. I had a conversation with a friend who said, 'I know we're taught that Christ is always with us – but it's really hard for me to understand how that relates to my job. I feel that when I get to work I leave Jesus at the door of my office building and then meet him on my way home.'

I appreciated the honesty of the comment and suspect that my friend is not alone in his feelings. When we are in a church service or homegroup, where the vocabulary could be described as *Christianspeak*, it all seems natural – but for many of us the world of work is a universe away. The only time Jesus gets a mention is as an expletive we wish could be deleted.

> **When I get to work I leave Jesus at the door.**

The Bible paints an altogether different picture. God is far from absent from the world and is concerned with life outside church programmes. We discover from the Bible that he is *omnipresent* (present everywhere), *omniscient* (all knowing) and *omnipotent* (all powerful). He is involved in the world that he made twenty-four hours a day, seven days a week. And the Gospels tell of Jesus engaging with real life. His teaching was packed with everyday stories of normal life, his friends were working men and women and his activities brought him into contact with real people in a real world.

I have a vivid childhood memory of seeing my class teacher out shopping. I was shocked to see Mrs King walking along the road with a man, and *they were holding hands*! I had no concept that teachers like Mrs King had any life outside school. I thought that on Fridays the cleaners put them away in cupboards with the PE equipment and someone brought them out again on a Monday.

I have a hunch that some Christians believe similar things about Jesus.

So why do some of us feel that we 'leave Jesus at the door' when it comes to our work?

It stems from our tendency to put life into compartments and not see it as a whole. So we make the division between spiritual activities (church things, Christian friends and events) and the rest of life. Another way of describing this division is as a split between the *sacred* and the *secular* – with the underlying assumption that God is interested in one, but not the other.

Abraham Kuyper, who was a brilliant theologian and politician (he was once the Dutch prime minister, and founded the Free University of Amsterdam), wrote these words:

> There is no area of our lives where the Lord Jesus does not put his hand on it and say – 'Mine!'

He was reflecting the teaching of the New Testament that discipleship is about the whole of life, not just part of it. We are going to look at one passage from a letter in the New Testament that illustrates this point. Take a few minutes to read Colossians 3:1 – 4:1 and make a note of some of the topics covered.

The congregation in Colossae would have gathered to hear Paul's letter read out loud. It would probably have been read as a whole – not in small bite-size chunks as we tend to do these days. The main theme of the letter could be summed up as *Jesus is all you need*. It seems that the young church had been influenced by the suggestion that faith in Christ was not enough and that, for someone to be a proper Christian, other mystical experiences were required.

Paul tackled this head on and made it clear that there is no-one like Jesus – he is Lord of everything and in him all the treasures of wisdom and knowledge are found. Nothing can be added or removed from his death and resurrection. He has triumphed over all the principalities and powers that lie behind the evil in our world. In Jesus Christ alone can salvation be found.

In this section of the letter Paul explains what discipleship entails. As I read through this passage, I made the following notes as I tried to gain an overview of what Paul passed on to his fellow Christians in Colossae.

3:1–4
Get your focus straight. I need to fix my mind on the things of God and not be preoccupied with things that won't last.

3:5–11
Strip off the old clothes (habits and attitudes) that represent the way I used to live.

3:12–14
Instead, put on the new clothes (habits and attitudes) that fit someone who has been touched by God's grace.

3:15–17
Be worshipping and thankful people.

3:18–21
Live as a faithful disciple of Christ at home – not just at church.

3:22 – 4:1
Live as a faithful disciple in my workplace too.

The thing that stands out most about the passage is that it treats the major compartments of my life as a whole. My personal life (ambition, values, behaviour and relationships), my family, my church and my work life are all covered in this explanation of what it means to follow Christ.

Key point
Christian discipleship is about the *whole* of our lives – not just the Sunday part.

Most of us are familiar with the expression 'so heavenly minded but no earthly use', and we could fall into the trap of thinking that is what Paul advocates when he writes:

Set your minds on things above, not on earthly things.[2]

But the very fact that he goes on to explain that our faith must apply in the everyday world demonstrates that he was not encouraging a head-in-the-clouds approach to life, but the complete opposite. Paul has his feet on the ground.

The famous writer G. K. Chesterton once described life before coming to faith in Christ as being like a man with his head in the sand, his legs kicking wildly in the air. What seems real to him is the earth – because his head is buried in it. When that individual comes to personal faith, God pulls him out of the sand. Christian men and women end up with their feet on the ground and their heads in the heavens, able to see clearly where to go.

With this in mind, I want to look at the verses in this passage that teach about being a disciple of Christ in the workplace. In particular I want to address three basic questions:

- Who is my boss?
- What is my job?
- How should I tackle my work?

Who is my boss?

Paul writes about slaves and masters,[3] which seems so far removed from our experience. It is like visiting a museum that exhibits long-redundant machines and appliances from another age. We may be fascinated by how people used to live, but these things have nothing to offer us in our modern world.

But the principles Paul teaches apply in every age, whether we use the language of slave / master or employee / boss. We may be more familiar with the latter style of language, but at the time Paul wrote this letter slavery was part of the fabric of the Roman-dominated world. It has been estimated that around the time Paul wrote his letter as much as a third of the population of Rome was made up of slaves. People became slaves through circumstances – often being captured as prisoners of war[4] – or through being unable to pay debts or being abandoned as children. Some were sentenced to a life of slavery as punishment for crime, others were born into slavery simply following the miserable life of their parents. We may feel that our twenty-first-century world is a better place, but sadly it is not and slavery is still a flourishing business around the world.[5]

When Paul wrote to the church in Colossae, there were both slaves and masters in the congregation. Paul reminds the slaves who is the ultimate boss:

> Whatever you do, work at it with all your heart, as working for the Lord, not for human masters, since you know that you will receive an inheritance from the Lord as a reward. It is the Lord Christ you are serving.[6]

Slave owners face an equally challenging call:

> Masters, provide your slaves with what is right and fair, because you know that you also have a Master in heaven.[7]

This was revolutionary stuff. In a world where slaves had no legal rights and were treated as pieces of property, Paul set out a level playing field. Master and slave should face their world of work as servants of Jesus first and foremost.

It is also revolutionary stuff in our culture, which feeds us the lie that you are what you earn or what you can buy. It does not matter if your name is on the door, or at the top of the notepaper, or if you don't have a paid job with a fancy title and fringe benefits. For his followers – whatever their work – Jesus is the ultimate boss.

For his followers – whatever their work – Jesus is the ultimate boss.

Ray Kroc, founder of the burger chain McDonald's, is quoted as saying: 'I speak of faith in McDonald's as if it were a religion. I believe in God, the family and McDonald's, and in the office the order is reversed.' That helps me understand my friend who believes that he leaves Jesus at the door when he starts work. But, according to Paul, that is lousy theology! You can't leave Jesus at the door if he's the boss.

The story is told of an elderly lady suffering from dementia. She had been a Christian for many years and knew the Bible well and it brought her great comfort. But, as her condition worsened, she began to lose the ability to recall things. Her favourite verse, which she knew off by heart, was this:

> Yet I am not ashamed, because I know whom I have believed, and am convinced that he is able to guard what I have entrusted to him for that day.[8]

It was a comfort to her just to recall this verse and think deeply about it. But, as her mind began to deteriorate, she could not remember all of it, until all that she could remember was 'he is able to guard what I have entrusted to him for that day'. In the last few weeks of her life, as her mind and body began to fail, the only word she could remember was 'him'. Towards the last hours of her life, she muttered the word over and over again. Every few moments, she would just say, 'Him, him, him.' Medically they may have judged that she had lost the plot, but personally I think she had found it.

For some of us who are struggling hard at work at the moment, the simple issue is that we have forgotten who the boss is.

Him.

Key point
No matter what your role, job title or salary bracket is, if you are a child of God then Jesus is your boss.

What is my job?
Questionnaires often contain an enquiry about our occupation. When we are introduced to someone it will not be long before the question comes up: 'What do you do?'

If you had to describe your work right now, what would you say? If you are not in paid employment it may be difficult to describe all that fills your day in caring for children, nursing a sick friend or doing a host of things to serve others.

But as a Christian, if Jesus is the boss, how can I describe my job?

To help us find the answer, I want to look briefly at another letter in the New Testament and consider what Paul says to the Christians in Corinth.

Nevertheless, each of you should retain the place in life that the Lord has assigned you and to which God has *called* you.

This is the rule I lay down in all the churches. Was a man already circumcised when he was *called*? He should not become uncircumcised. Was a man uncircumcised when he was *called*? He should not be circumcised. Circumcision is nothing and uncircumcision is nothing. Keeping God's commands is what counts. Each of you should remain in the situation which you were in when God *called* you. Were you a slave when you were *called*? Don't let it trouble you – although if you can gain your freedom, do so. For those who were slaves when *called* by the Lord are the Lord's freed people; similarly, those who were free when *called* are Christ's slaves. You were bought at a price; do not become slaves of people. Brothers and sisters, all of you, as responsible to God, should remain in the situation in which God *called* you.[9]

Note that I have emphasized the word *called*, which is used by Paul eight times in the space of a few verses. This passage might seem a bit confusing at first – particularly the reference to circumcision and uncircumcision. But what Paul is saying is this: beyond the change of becoming a follower of Christ, don't try to change who you are. If you are a Jew, if that is your background, then do not deny your culture, even now that you have become a Christian. And if you are a Gentile, do not deny that culture – that is your background. If you are a slave, if you get the chance to be free, take it, but do not think that these peripheral things are terribly important to God. The important thing is that you are a child of God and God has called you. Live life in the light of that calling above all else.

Interestingly, the word *called* is linked to the word for church. The word *church* in the Greek language is *ecclesia* (from which we get words such as ecclesiastical) and it simply means *God's called-out people*. So what Paul is really getting at here is this: I am *called* to be a child of God, I am *called* to live as a disciple of Christ, and that, in a sense, is my ultimate 'job'. So, to be strictly accurate, the next time I am faced with the word 'Occupation' on a form, I could write 'full-time disciple of Jesus Christ'.

In the English language, we make a distinction between a *vocation* (which comes from a Latin word meaning *calling*) and a *job*. Unlike a paid job, which you might be doing just to pay the rent, a vocation means that there is a sense in which you have an ambition, a call, to go into that particular field of work. Now that's a very Christian idea: our vocation, our calling, is to live as disciples of Christ, although our actual jobs may change from time to time.

> **Our jobs may change, but our calling in Christ remains the same.**

I think that this gives a sense of value and worth to those of us who struggle. It may be that ill health prevents you from having a salaried job, or it may be that you're retired and no longer in paid employment, or perhaps you are reading this as someone who would love to have full-time work but current circumstances make that impossible. Look carefully at what the scripture says: your vocation is that you are called by God to be his child, his son, his daughter, and a follower of Christ. Our jobs may change, our circumstances of work may differ, but our calling in Christ remains the same.

This is why it is very important to know that we are in the job God wants us to be in. I have been amazed to meet Christians who will move their family from one side of the world to the other to change their job, but they will not even think of praying about it or sharing it with people who care for them pastorally. That is compartmentalized Christianity rearing its head once again. God is pushed to the margins, and it is the opposite of 'minding heavenly things'. If our attitude is, 'Here's my chance to make more money, to climb up the ladder,' we are missing the best. If we are minding heavenly things, we view things differently. A job is a job, but our vocation is a calling to be a child of God.

Returning to Paul and his teaching to the church at Colossae, let's recall his words:

> Whatever you do, work at it with all your heart, as working for the Lord, not for human masters.[10]

Note that Paul says, '*Whatever* you do . . .' We should not say that some jobs are important and others are not. Paul says that *whatever* your job is at the moment, whether or not it has a name or a salary attached to it, your vocation is to live it out as a child of God. Surely, you might say, this is an unreal expectation: you cannot live in the world of work with this attitude and survive. But we are urged to 'work at it with all your heart'. You show me a boss who would not give his right arm to have somebody who worked wholeheartedly. That is motivation of the highest order.

There was a manager in a factory who was visited by a time and motion expert, who asked, 'How many people work here?' The boss replied, 'About half of them!'

There's a true story told of Charles Haddon Spurgeon (1834–92), the famous Baptist preacher, pastor of the Metropolitan Tabernacle in London. In those days, when you applied to become a member of the church you were interviewed by the minister and all the deacons and elders – a terrifying ordeal! Just imagine sitting in front of a group of Victorian men with long faces sporting bushy sideburns and beards and wearing their formal suits complete with watch and chain.

A teenage girl who worked as a maid in a big London house had applied for church membership. After she was ushered in and sat down, Charles Spurgeon asked, 'What evidence can you offer that you have truly repented of your sins and are trusting Christ?'

The nervous girl thought for a moment and then replied, 'Well, I have stopped sweeping the dirt under the rugs when I clean the house.'

Spurgeon then said, 'No further questions. We'll receive her! Give her the right hand of fellowship.'

That is what it means to tackle your daily work for the Lord – with all your heart.

Key point
My vocation/calling is to live as a disciple of Christ.

How should I tackle my work?

The world of work throws up many challenges. Paul spells out four guiding principles that offer some direction as we consider living as a follower of Christ in the workplace.

1. Be obedient

Slaves, obey your earthly masters in everything.

Does that really mean *everything*? Sometimes we are faced with difficult choices, moral dilemmas, and that's where the Caesar principle comes in. Jesus was once asked if it was right to pay taxes to Caesar. He replied: 'Give to Caesar what is Caesar's, and to God what is God's.'[11]

Caesar is due what is his by law, but as soon as he begins

to demand what belongs to God we have the right to say, 'Hands off.' If you are asked to do something at work that you know is wrong, you should refuse. It may be time to quit the job, or your refusal may lead to your losing the job. You would not be the first person to face that. But this first principle is clear: obedience to the company rules, the boss's standards or government legislation is one way in which we demonstrate our commitment to Christ.

2. Be honest

And do it, not only when their eye is on you and to win their favour, but with sincerity of heart and reverence for the Lord.

It is easy to work well when we are being watched, but how do we perform when no-one is watching?

As a minister I am regularly asked to supply references and sometimes I am asked specific questions about the candidate's honesty, reliability, punctuality and ability to get on with others. According to Paul, moral uprightness is about how we are at work when no-one is watching. That covers personal phone calls, stationery, expenses claims, giving accurate reports on what is happening and owning up when something has gone wrong.

For a Christian, honesty is more than the best policy – it's the only one.

3. Be hard-working

Whatever you do, work at it with all your heart.

'*All* your heart' means give it your very, very best. Putting it simply, we need to aim to be the best that we can be. I may not be the brightest or most experienced at my job, but Christ's call on my life draws me out to be the most committed.

Many have enjoyed the music of Oscar Hammerstein, of Rodgers and Hammerstein fame. He wrote a book entitled *Lyrics* and in it tells a story that gives an insight into the high standards he applied to his work.

> **We need to aim to be the best that we can be.**

He once saw a photograph of the Statue of Liberty taken from a helicopter. What struck Hammerstein was the elaborate detail in the statue's hairstyle – even though helicopters did not exist when the sculptor made it. He could not have known that one day people would fly over it and view his work from the top so closely, yet he put in as much work into the bits that were hidden as he did into the bits that were seen. Hammerstein wrote:

> When you are creating a work of art, or any other kind of work, finish the job off perfectly. You never know when a helicopter or some other instrument not at the moment invented may come along and find you out.

There is nothing wrong in taking a pride in our work – in fact, quite the opposite. At creation, 'God saw that it was good'. We can take a pride in our work and offer it as worship to the God in whose image we have been made.

4. Be fair

Note that little phrase tucked into Paul's teaching on the world of work:

> . . . there is no favouritism.[12]

God does not look differently at so-called fat cats and people on benefits. He is not swayed by which tax bracket we find ourselves in. And those who have responsibility for others are warned:

> Masters, provide your slaves with what is right and fair, because you know that you also have a Master in heaven.[13]

This includes those of us who have responsibility for others – their welfare, pay and working conditions. You may not be a boss, but you may be managing people, and we are called to be fair in our judgments, fair in our decisions and fair in our dealings with people, seeking to be righteous in the decisions that we make, remembering that we have a Master in heaven to whom we are accountable.

Key point
To tackle my work well as a disciple of Christ, I need to aim continually at *obedience*, *honesty*, *hard work* and *fairness*.

From the pen of Hudson Taylor, the great missionary pioneer of another generation, comes the cat and dog test. This is what he wrote:

> If your mother and father, your sister and brother, if the very cat and dog in your house, are not happier because you are a Christian, it is a question whether you really are one.

Perhaps a statement Paul made earlier in his letter to the Colossians might help us to carry Jesus into our world of work rather than leave him at the door.

And whatever you do, whether in word or deed, do it all in
the name of the Lord Jesus, giving thanks to God the Father
through him.[14]

Whatever you do. No room there for 'I'm just a homemaker'.
It says 'whatever you do'. Whatever you do in the world of
work this week – driving a bus, dictating letters, going to
court, putting your arm around someone who cries, helping
children with their homework – *whatever* you do, do it all in
the name of the Lord Jesus, giving thanks to God the Father
through him.

Here's a suggestion: why not write that verse out? Put
it on a postcard, put it on the shaving mirror, put it by the
draining board, stick it on your dashboard. Put it on your
computer screen as a constant reminder. Perhaps the reference is enough: *Colossians 3:17*. However you write it, or
wherever you put it, learn it, pray it and let it become part of
your life.

You see, my friend was wrong in his assumption that he
could leave Jesus at the entrance to his workplace. You can't
leave Jesus anywhere, because he is *everywhere*.

If we make that discovery, we will find something that will
revolutionize the way we view our world, live our lives and
face our daily work.

For further thought . . .

1. How would you help the man who said he left Jesus at the door of his office find a different view?

2. How does the idea that 'Jesus is my boss' affect the way you look at your daily work?

3. Consider the four guidelines that help us to 'think Christianly' about work:
   - Obedience
   - Honesty
   - Hard work
   - Fairness

   Can you identify some specific ways in which these values can make a difference to the way you tackle your job?

3. I HATE MY JOB!

In one of the churches where I served as pastor we made a special focus on the workplace. We encouraged people to share some of the pressures they were facing in their jobs. We invited them to fill in a card sharing specific needs for prayer. This involved a commitment and an invitation.

The commitment was that our prayer team would specifically pray that week for every need listed on each card. The invitation was for the person who wrote the card to pray each day for his or her own specific request. The challenge was to bring God into the workplace and the prayer requests revealed a list of very different needs.

Please pray that as a mum with three small children I will feel what I do is important.

Pray that I will make the right decision this week over the future of several staff.

Pray that I will be able to get on with X, who makes my life miserable.

Please pray we win the contract.

Prayers, please, as I am looking after my wife who has senile dementia – that I will have lots of love and patience.

Please pray I will find a job after two years of being redundant.

Can you pray that Class 4f settle down and that I am able to win their respect.

I need prayer to speak up about something at work that is wrong and I don't have much courage.

I need to be more open about my faith.

Asking that I may feel happier in my work and that what I do is worthwhile.

Help me to be more pleasant in dealing with the customers – especially the grumpy ones.

Pray that I will survive OFSTED inspection and not be stressed out.

The response and the results were remarkable. Although most of the prayer requests were anonymous (for obvious reasons), a number of people shared answers to prayer. Some had never prayed about their jobs in any specific way before. Difficult decisions, awkward colleagues and demanding deadlines simply hadn't figured as important when it came to prayer requests. As one man expressed it, 'This has totally transformed the way I look at my job!'

I think the abiding lesson we all learned was that God was interested in all of life, not just the church bits. And it encouraged us to pray for one another in the workplace.

Key point
God can make a difference at our places of work.

Wrong job?

But what do we do when we find ourselves feeling genuinely unhappy at work?

I shared a meal with a man who felt trapped in his job. He was successful at what he did and earned a good salary, but he lived with the gnawing doubt that he should be doing something else. We talked about guidance and gifts and how to discover satisfaction in mundane things. But I came away with the impression that here was someone seeking God's call to something better when he had already got the call.

Perhaps you are currently unhappy in your work, but you cannot put your finger on the reason for your dissatisfaction. The main question you should ask is this: 'Am I where God has put me?' The answer to that question will determine what action you need to take.

For some, they know they are in the right job, but the pressure is hard to handle. Others point to specific struggles with demands and expectations of colleagues. Some would say they have hit a plateau and work holds no job satisfaction any more. Each of these issues is understandable and the problems are not insoluble. But the fundamental issue remains to discover whether we are in the place God has planted us.

When Tony Blair was British prime minister, he spent a morning on a back-to-work computer course in his constituency along with members of the general public. This was a golden photo opportunity and, as cameras and journalists jostled for pictures, Blair noticed that the man at the next desk looked uncomfortable. He reassured him, 'Forget who I am and ignore this lot.'

His neighbour thanked him and replied, 'That's not what's bothering me. What I'm worried about is that on every test on this computer I'm getting the right answers and I can see you're getting the wrong ones. But I'm unemployed and you're the prime minister!'

There are some questions we cannot answer. And some things we face don't seem to make sense – at least not immediately.

What do we do when we reach the conclusion that we are simply in the wrong job?

I preached a sermon recently with the title 'Faith in the Storm'. One of my congregation e-mailed me a few days later and said, 'I'm not so much in a storm as becalmed. Nothing is happening – help!'

This may describe you at present. Things in your work life are going nowhere and you desperately want out. Let me suggest some steps that may offer a way forward.

Write down what you are struggling with

Putting things down on paper can help to clear our thinking. What specific things in your current work make you frustrated, angry, bored, unfulfilled? Have you always felt this way, or have things happened that have changed your view? Are there individuals with whom you find it difficult to work? In what ways does your attitude towards them need to change?

> **Putting things down on paper can help to clear our thinking.**

Write down what would be an ideal job for you

Don't be afraid to dream, and picture those things that you believe would fit your skills and experience. Think about what would be an ideal job for you and list some of the reasons why it would be a good move. If you can't think of a specific job, just list the things you would want included in an ideal job.

Get some really good advice

That may be from a career counsellor, a pastor, or a colleague or friend you trust and respect. It may even be your current boss! You might know someone in the kind of job you would like to do – try approaching that person for advice. Don't just sit there feeling discontented. Take positive steps.

Pray

Bring God into your workplace and ask some friends in your church or homegroup to pray with you and for you. It is not a bad thing to set some kind of time limit so that things don't drag on too long. Focus your prayers during this time and let others know what you are doing so that they can pray for you.

Feeling stuck is not comfortable, but be encouraged by those who have been there themselves and have made a fulfilling change in their work life. I remember a conversation with Sue, a young woman in our church. She felt totally trapped in her fairly mundane job and was aware that her parents (who had helped fund her through university) wanted her to get a proper job and develop her career. Sue was juggling with some conflicting priorities and one of the first things we needed to work on was sorting out the tangle this caused. Without any disrespect to her mum and dad, Sue saw the need to set her own career path as a Christian. What mattered most was what God wanted for her. Months later, she settled into a new job that she found suited her gifts and, what is more, her parents were totally happy with her decision.

Right job, wrong attitude?

I was sitting in a meeting alongside several colleagues from work, listening intently as the speaker was introduced. He started with what was (for me at least) an embarrassing question. 'Hands up if you are in a place you don't want to be and doing a job that you don't want to do.' The truth was, I was so desperately unhappy in my job that I wanted to put up both hands and wave my legs in the air as well.

But I didn't.

I didn't do it because I was a coward and I wanted to avoid having to answer awkward questions from colleagues.

I certainly wanted to hear what the speaker had to say, however.

The topic was the biblical story of Daniel, which we are going to look at in some detail because it is all about a very difficult situation. The speaker made the case that Daniel was probably living where he didn't want to be and doing what he didn't want to do, but somehow he found meaning and purpose in his life.

I had never read the story of Daniel in that way before. I thought it was all lions' den and fiery furnace and a million miles away from finding God's grace in a mundane job. How little I knew, and how much there was to discover.

> **Even when work is a drag, there are ways to handle it positively.**

If the story of Daniel teaches us anything, it is that we can find grace in difficult circumstances and seemingly impossible jobs. Even when work is a drag, there are ways to handle it positively.

Daniel's circumstances

Daniel's name means 'God is my judge', so bound up in this was his family faith. He was a Jew and lived in Judah in the city of Jerusalem some 600 years before Jesus Christ was born. He came from a well-connected family from what some would call an upper-class background.

Daniel was born at a very turbulent time. The nation of Assyria had been the dominant power, but they were losing their position to the Babylonians, whose empire would become the prevailing world power for some years to come. Egypt was militarily strong and Judah – Daniel's nation – were vassals of the Egyptians. They paid tribute, or tax as we would describe it today, and the Babylonians decided that this vassal state of Judah should come under their control. This was all part of the Babylonian plan to establish themselves as the supreme world power, and military victories over the Assyrians and Egyptians meant that few were left to argue.

This is the background to the opening statement in the book of Daniel:

> In the third year of the reign of Jehoiakim king of Judah, Nebuchadnezzar king of Babylon came to Jerusalem and besieged it.[1]

This puts the date of the first Babylonian attack around the year 605 BC, and it led to the first of three deportations that left the city of Jerusalem and its temple in ruins. Daniel was caught in the crossfire and became embroiled in King Nebuchadnezzar's brutal subjugation policy. This involved taking the top layer of Jewish society to his capital city, Babylon. A puppet king was left in place, but the people of power and influence were taken away. Daniel and his friends were part of the brain drain to Babylon, uprooted from all they knew and loved, and forced to live in an alien culture.

It is hard to imagine what this must have meant to Daniel, who was probably a teenager when he saw his nation and his world fall apart. As well as taking people, Nebuchadnezzar took treasures from the temple and put them in the shrine of the god he worshipped in Babylon. By doing this he was making a powerful statement about which god was the greatest. And Daniel, his family and friends had to come to terms with this challenge to their faith.

Nebuchadnezzar's battle was for hearts and minds, which explains his instruction that the brightest and best of the young Jews should be singled out for special treatment. Daniel and his three friends were chosen for their potential and selected to undergo an intensive period of training. Their names were changed, and an attempt was made to change their culture too. Babylonian language, history and literature lessons were to fill their young lives for the next three years. And during this time they would be kept on the finest diet from the king's kitchens. Nebuchadnezzar's policy had two clear aims: first, to rob the conquered nation of its brightest and best and, second, to raise a new generation reprogrammed and desperately loyal to their new masters.

Daniel appears to have lived through all of the seventy years of exile his people experienced in Babylon. But whatever Nebuchadnezzar had in mind, it didn't work with Daniel. Far from being subsumed by Babylonian culture, Daniel remained clear both in his faith and in his focus. This did not hold back his development within the Babylonian civil service, however, and he became a trusted adviser to three kings and was a man with a strong reputation for integrity. The abiding lesson of his life is that he found God in a hard place. Perhaps a more accurate way of expressing it would be to say that God found him and worked through him in that hard place.

Reading his story, we learn that Daniel was a man of principle (he learned to swim against the tide), a man of prayer (which was the key to his extraordinary life) and a man of prophecy (some fulfilled in his lifetime, some fulfilled in Jesus and some yet to be fulfilled).

For those of us who struggle with our circumstances or find ourselves in a job that is less than fulfilling, we find Daniel an inspiration. Here was someone who was possibly:

- living in a place he didn't want to be;
- working for a man he didn't want to serve;
- tackling a job he didn't want to do.

Some would point out that Daniel achieved a powerful position in the Babylonian court and no doubt enjoyed a comfortable lifestyle. Life turned out well for him, so to talk of him being in a difficult situation may appear strange. But, remember, we can read the whole story. When he was uprooted and deported as a teenager, Daniel had no idea how it would end. He made the most of it and found fulfilment on the way, but I don't think being a political prisoner was his first choice in life.

The ultimate authority lay in God's hands.

There is much debate about who wrote the book of Daniel and the date when it was written, but there is a telling phrase at the very beginning. Whether it came from Daniel's pen or not, his life tells that he believed what was written:

And the Lord delivered Jehoiakim king of Judah into his hand . . . [2]

Daniel came to see that the disaster that befell his people was within God's plan. Nebuchadnezzar may have been in office, but he was not in power. The ultimate authority lay in God's hands. A preacher of another generation wrote a book on Daniel with the subtitle 'The Persistent Government of God in the Government of the World'.[3]

That was a foundational belief for Daniel and it helped him to view his circumstances with faith. He knew he was where he was because God had put him there and that helped him to find meaning in what would otherwise have seemed a meaningless situation.

Key point
If I know I am in the place where God has put me, then I can view my circumstances with faith.

Daniel's dedication

Daniel not only survived Babylon, he thrived there. And reading his story, we discover the extraordinary dedication to God that shielded him from the powerful pull to conform to the prevailing culture. P. T. Forsyth made the astute observation:

> If *within* us we find nothing *over* us we succumb to what is *around* us.[4]

Over Daniel's life – and that of his three friends – was a devotion to Yahweh, the God of their fathers, that would stand the test of a fiery furnace and a den of lions. This is demonstrated by two principles that fashioned Daniel's character.

1. He guarded his heart

The book of Proverbs is rich with wisdom and one of its gems reveals:

> Above all else, guard your heart,
>   for it is the wellspring of life.[5]

Daniel's dedication to guarding his heart is seen at the start of the story when he refused the rich food and wine from

King Nebuchadnezzar's table. This was not food faddism. Although there is a disagreement among scholars, it seems likely that Daniel and his friends refused the food for one of two reasons; they would not eat what was outside Jewish food laws. Also the first portions of the king's food and wine were routinely offered to the Babylonian gods. Daniel (with considerable diplomatic skill and charm) persuaded the royal official to give them ten days to prove their point by allowing them a strict diet confined to vegetables and water. They won both their case and the respect of the official and went on to be fit and healthy and also outstanding students.[6]

A telling phrase in this account reads:

> But Daniel resolved not to defile himself with the royal food and wine.[7]

Daniel made a resolution that certain things were non-negotiable and by laying down such markers he knew he would be able to chart his course. Guarding our hearts is easier to do when we have set boundaries and stick to them. For example, ambition, wealth, balance of work/life, career moves, relationships and personal integrity are just some of the areas where we would be wise to set boundaries early and check our position often.

Guarding our hearts is easier to do when we have set boundaries and stick to them.

Lois is a journalist who made a conscious choice early in her career that she would write stories that reflected the actual circumstances rather than resorting to speculation and rumour. She has worked with various bosses who have responded differently to her style. One in particular gave her a hard time for failing to be 'hard-nosed', as he put it. But Lois sees it differently. Her aims are fairness and accuracy and there is nothing soft about the stories she writes.

I recall a conversation with a man who was an accountant working for a company that owned a large group of garages. We were talking about faith and he told me, 'I have always believed it's impossible to be a Christian in the motor trade,' but he added that in his new job he was working for a boss who was well known as a committed Christian. He was deeply impressed with his boss's integrity and professional competence and told me that he had to rethink his assertion that you couldn't be a Christian in that line of business.

A. W. Tozer wrote, 'It is not what a man does that determines whether his work is sacred or secular. It is why he does it.' It is not whether you are a bricklayer or an evangelist; it is not whether you are a bank manger or a pastor. It is not what you do, it is why you are doing it.

Daniel's job description may have been 'senior adviser to King Nebuchadnezzar', but that would have been just a bit of paper. The job description in his heart was 'servant of God'.

What is the job description in your heart?

2. He guarded his habits

Mention the name Daniel, and those who know the story will link it with the lions' den – arguably the most famous episode in his whole life. But what put him in that dangerous position?[8]

Many years had passed by and a new king, Darius, who was a Mede, had taken the throne. Daniel had survived this regime change and had become part of the king's inner cabinet of three – which says much about his skill and value.

Some were jealous of Daniel's influence and tried to find ways to depose him. But there were no skeletons in the closet, nor was he susceptible to bribery or corruption. Those who wanted to see Daniel fall knew that the only way to trip him up would be in relation to his faith. They appealed to King Darius's proud, arrogant heart by suggesting that no-one should pray to any god for a whole month. The only object of prayer in that time should be Darius himself and this act of devotion would demonstrate that he was the greatest among men or gods.

Daniel, however, had a well-known routine of praying three times a day with his windows open, facing his beloved Jerusalem. Even as a busy royal official this daily ritual continued openly and when the decree was issued he saw no reason to change what had become, literally, the habit of a lifetime.

Those who hated Daniel lost no time in telling the king that this foreigner had shown his true colours by refusing to obey the royal edict. Much to Darius's distress, Daniel was thrown to the lions. The king tried everything to save his most loyal servant from this fate, but it ended in failure and Daniel bravely faced death. God delivered him, and this resulted in a remarkable open letter from the king to the furthest corners of his empire praising the God of Daniel and acknowledging:

> For he is the living God
>   and he endures for ever;
> his kingdom will not be destroyed,
>   his dominion will never end.[9]

Daniel made a conscious choice in his career and it was a choice that he reaffirmed at various points. He determined that he would not be defined by the character of his circumstances, but by the content of his character. He guarded his godly habits and by so doing nurtured his faith.

People can easily lose the ability to do this. As they climb the ladder of success, they begin to compromise and cut corners. Good habits fade and bad habits flourish as power, influence and wealth increase. That is why, as disciples of Christ, we need to form relationships where we can practise accountability by encouraging others to speak into our lives. Sadly, for some, as the success and responsibility increase, their spiritual moorings loosen. They don't set out to deny their faith: it is simply superseded by more pressing things. Travel, business meetings and the pressure of the treadmill of success work together to push the routines of godly habits to the margins. Church attendance becomes less frequent and there is little time to develop relationships with others who share the family faith – and before long the icy tentacles of nominalism freeze once-warm hearts.

Daniel's story stands as a lighthouse of hope and teaches us that you can live a godly life in a godless world.

Key point
Guarding my heart and my habits are two principles that shape a godly character.

Daniel's progress

Some struggle with their job because they can see little spiritual value attached. The same could have been true of Daniel, as much of his life was spent oiling the wheels of power for two empires. His daily tasks could at times have seemed fairly meaningless compared to the realm of faith. But at various points of the story he had opportunities to see a higher value and recognize that he had a part to play in a bigger plan. He experienced the favour of God in his life, including the seemingly mundane, irrelevant parts. And in it all he found the pathway that God had marked out for him.

Knowing God's favour

At the beginning of the story we are told that Daniel and his three friends showed exceptional abilities and that this was a direct result of God's gifting in their lives. Their intellectual capacity was a sign of God's favour.[10]

Later, when Daniel offered to interpret King Nebuchadnezzar's dream in difficult circumstances, he leaves no room for doubt that he knew where his skills came from. There is no ambiguity in his statement:

> No wise man, enchanter, magician or diviner can explain to the king the mystery he has asked about, but there is a God in heaven who reveals mysteries.[11]

Daniel didn't lose sight of where his gifting came from. We would do well to remember that our skills and ability to work are gifts from God and signs of his favour. Daniel was heeding the instruction given in the law of Moses about having a humble heart when it came to work and wealth:

> **Our skills and ability to work are gifts from God.**

> You may say to yourself, 'My power and the strength of my hands have produced this wealth for me.' But remember the LORD your God, for it is he who gives you the ability to produce wealth . . . [12]

Learning to live with a sense of God's favour can lead to a transformation in our attitude to the routine of our working lives. Consciously thanking God for our gifts, the ability to work and the skill to earn money lifts worship into the marketplace and offers a new way of looking at the daily routine.

Finding God's pathway

Most of us have discovered that our attitude governs how much we enjoy or dislike something. If we set out with a negative attitude, it will colour the way we tackle a particular task.

Think of Daniel faced with a lifetime sentence to live in a foreign court. However comfortable his surroundings and influential his position, it was probably not where he wanted to be – but, as his story shows, he made a series of decisions that affected his attitude to his circumstances. As a result he found God's pathway for his life.

Our attitude lies at the heart of job satisfaction, or the lack of it. A well-known story illustrates the point.

When President Bill Clinton first met Nelson Mandela, they shared a memorable conversation. Clinton asked a searching question. 'When you were released from prison, Mr Mandela, I woke my daughter at three o'clock in the morning. I wanted her to see this historic event. As you marched from the cellblock across the yard to the gate of the prison, the camera focused in on your face. I have never seen such anger, and even hatred, in any man as was expressed on your face at that time. That's not the Nelson Mandela I know today. What was that all about?'

Mandela replied, 'I'm surprised that you saw that, and I regret that the cameras caught my anger. As I walked across the courtyard that day I thought to myself, "They've taken everything from you that matters. Your cause is dead. Your family is gone. Your friends have been killed. Now they're releasing you, but there is nothing left for you out there." And I hated them for what they had taken from me. Then I sensed an inner voice saying to me, "Nelson! For twenty-seven years you were their prisoner, but you were always a free man! Don't allow them to make you into a free man, only to turn you into their prisoner!" '

Mandela knew that the choice was his to make and, as his infectious smile and cheerful spirit revealed, he chose well.

We can choose how we feel about our world of work. We can waste our lives by wishing we were someone else or somewhere else, or, like Daniel, we can find God where we are.

Key point
Knowing God's favour and finding God's pathway should be the driving influences in my life.

For further thought . . .

1. What are some of the pressures you are facing in your work? How would you phrase these as specific prayer requests?

2. What lessons from Daniel's life are most applicable and helpful to you at this moment?

3. In what ways can you better guard your heart and your habits?

4. 'ON YER BIKE!'

Sometimes words and phrases take on a life of their own. Norman Tebbit, a close political ally of Margaret Thatcher, Britain's first woman prime minister, made a famous speech about over-dependence on the welfare state. He cited the example of his father, who had been made redundant during a recession. Tebbit forcefully pointed out that his father didn't wait for people to rush around and help, but got on his bike to look for work. Suddenly, 'On yer bike!' became a headline, a soundbite, an instantly recognizable phrase. It became a piece of shorthand in a sometimes heated debate. Whatever the merits or otherwise of that specific political point, most would agree that those who can help themselves need to do just that.

Strange as it may seem, there was at least one newly planted church in New Testament times where lazing around had become an art form – the church in Thessalonica. The apostle Paul, in writing to the Thessalonians, was hardly likely to use the phrase 'on yer bike', but his message came to the same thing, as we will see.

There is no doubt that idleness is not good for us. I have had the privilege of being in pastoral leadership in several churches and, from first-hand observation, I concur with the apostle Paul that Christians need to work for their bread and butter. Some Christians simply don't have enough to do and fill their time with things that are ultimately a waste of time. There are clear parallels between the twenty-first century and the first century.

Thessalonica

In the first century, the city of Thessalonica was the provincial capital and boasted the finest natural harbour in the Aegean Sea, ideal for trade and a draw for visitors. The city was multicultural and multifaith. Its thriving business community gave birth to many trade guilds, each providing a constant stream of dinners and banquets linked to the worship of a particular god or goddess. It is little surprise that Paul saw the strategic importance of the city and was responsible for planting a church there.[1]

He stayed only a short time, mainly due to a public riot caused by his preaching, but he left behind a young and inexperienced group of Christian disciples. Anxious for their welfare, he sent his colleague Timothy on a follow-up visit. He returned with positive news.[2] Paul wrote a letter to encourage his friends to be strong in their faith, recognizing that they faced many pressures which could discourage and deflect them. He wrote a second letter to the church just a few months later, very much along the same lines, although there were a few pastoral issues he decided to address. One particular problem had to do with a wrong attitude to work held by some of the congregation.

A pastoral problem

It is easy to make mistakes when starting out on something new. Certain members of the congregation at Thessalonica were simply not willing to work. Paul had to write some strong words in his second letter:

> In the name of the Lord Jesus Christ, we command you, brothers and sisters, to keep away from every believer who is idle and does not live according to the teaching you received from us.[3]

It is important to note that these were people who *would* not work, as opposed to people who *could* not work. The reasons were not to do with ill health or special circumstances. These people just did not want to work.

Paul had already highlighted this issue in his previous letter:

> Make it your ambition to lead a quiet life, to mind your own business and to work with your hands, just as we told you, so that your daily life may win the respect of outsiders and so that you will not be dependent on anybody.[4]

It has been suggested that some new believers enjoyed the idea of fellowship meals, an activity that was widely practised by Christians wherever new churches were springing up. The *agapé* meal celebrated the death and resurrection of Jesus in the Eucharist when bread and wine were offered and when Christians shared food in a communal meal. For poorer members, it may well have been the best meal of the week and a time when the church expressed family solidarity and care. Some, it seems, chose not to work to earn their keep, but relied on the hospitality and generosity of others. Fellowship meals provided a free lunch ticket and some were content to live this way.

Another contributing factor may have been some odd ideas surrounding the return of Jesus, another of the issues Paul touched on in both his letters. People in the congregation may have been so caught up with the idea of Jesus coming back that they could not be bothered to work for a living. Their attitude was, 'If this is all going to end, then what's the point?'

Others have suggested that this reluctance to work may be connected with the social conditions in Thessalonica, where patronage was a part of life.[5] Patrons sponsored people who were further down the social scale. Such people were not expected to work for their keep, but were meant to wait in attendance on their benefactors and sing their praises. In

> **New life in Christ demanded a new lifestyle.**

the social pecking order, the more clients you sponsored as a patron, the greater your status within the community. Those who take this view see Paul challenging the people who were caught up in such an unproductive lifestyle and warning them of the danger of becoming busybodies involved in trivial pursuits.[6] They may have chosen to live under the privilege of a patron in their pre-Christian days, but their new life in Christ demanded a new lifestyle.

A pastoral prescription

Whatever the root cause of this pastoral problem, Paul tackles it in three ways: by *example*, *teaching* and *discipline*.

Example

Paul reminded them of how he behaved during the short time he was in their city. He and his team paid their way and covered their overheads without cost to the congregation. Paul was a tentmaker and would find business for his trade wherever he went, and he and his team were steadfast in their determination to offer the good news about Jesus free of charge.[7] But there was a point behind the principle:

> We were not idle when we were with you, nor did we eat anyone's food without paying for it. On the contrary, we worked night and day, labouring and toiling so that we would not be a burden to any of you. We did this, not because we

do not have the right to such help, but in order to make ourselves a model for you to follow.[8]

Example is always the best teacher, and Paul and his team had set out to demonstrate that the Christian faith was about giving, not sponging.

Teaching

Paul had laid down some clear guidelines for these believers and he reminds them of one of the lessons in his nurture course for new disciples:

> For even when we were with you, we gave you this rule: 'If a man will not work, he shall not eat.'[9]

He is tackling what we might describe as a theology of work. In the first century there was no welfare state – so if you were sick or unable to work, you could only rely on family or close friends to help. The first Christian communities extended the concept of family and set out to care for their own vulnerable members. In such a care culture, it would be relatively easy to live off the kindness and hospitality of others in the congregation. In shared meals some would often take yet rarely give, and this is the point Paul highlights. If an individual refuses to work and contribute to the good of the community, then they should not partake in shared meals.

Idleness was not an option for serious disciples.

As one preacher eloquently expressed it: 'A fog in the pulpit leads to a mist in the pew.' In other words, if those who teach are not clear about what they believe, that adversely affects their hearers.

There was nothing foggy about Paul's instructions to the congregation at Thessalonica: idleness was not an option for serious disciples.

Discipline

What do you do if people simply refuse to listen to instruction? Paul is in no doubt as he writes his second letter to the believers in Thessalonica. He is concerned that some in the congregation have made an idol of being idle and have perhaps dreamed up a superspiritual excuse for their unwillingness to work. Instead of being legitimately busy, they have become mere busybodies. Paul warns:

> Such people we command and urge in the Lord Jesus Christ to settle down and earn the bread they eat.[10]

He anticipates that for some in the congregation this is a hard word and so adds a firm instruction:

> Take special note of those who do not obey our instruction in this letter. Do not associate with them, in order that they may feel ashamed. Yet do not regard them as enemies, but warn them as fellow believers.[11]

It is important to understand that Paul writes about discipline, not excommunication. But he clearly saw this issue as a major problem in Thessalonica and perhaps in other places as well.[12]

Lessons of life

There is a story about a man who went to the office early one morning, long before anyone else arrived. The phone rang, so he picked it up and the caller said that he wanted to talk to someone in the engineering department. The man replied, 'There's no-one here at the moment. You've called before the staff have arrived. But I'm here and I'll do the best I can to help you with your query. What is it?'

The line went quiet and the caller asked, 'What's your job there?'

The man replied, 'I'm the manager, actually.'

The caller said, 'OK, I'll call back later, as I want to speak to someone who knows what they're talking about.'

There are many books on management, leadership and best practice in business. They contain valuable insights and can help us in the task of continuous improvement. But the Bible is an extra-special source of wisdom. It is a book that knows what it is talking about.

Paul's pastoral dilemma at Thessalonica gives us insight into how to live productive lives and avoid the trap of lazy living. I want to suggest three lessons.

Lesson 1: God wants us to be useful, not idle

We are entrusted with life as a gift. Time is a precious commodity, a gift from God. Twenty-four hours in a day, 168 hours in a week, 8,736 hours in a year – we all live with the same measure of time. It's a gift from God, but how do we *use* it?

We may feel that we are productive in every way, but let me suggest two contemporary temptations to idleness.

> **Time is a precious commodity, a gift from God.**

First, television. How many hours does the average person spend slumped in front of the one-eyed god in the corner of the living room? I spoke with someone recently and mentioned a programme that had been on the TV that week. He told me he didn't have a television.

I asked why. 'It's a deliberate choice,' he replied. 'I know that I am by nature a time-waster and I know of nothing that uses up more time than the TV and therefore I don't even want to have it in the house.' I applaud his determination.

Second, what about personal interests? Now, they can be important as a means of relaxation or developing various skills. God wants us to have balanced lives and personal interests or hobbies can be good and healthy, but if they dominate our time they can draw us away from the really important things. It is possible to be idle by simply wasting too much time in activities that are not the best investment. There is a verse in the Old Testament that says:

Those who fear God will avoid all extremes.[13]

Being a workaholic is extreme, being idle is in the same category, and going overboard on a leisure-time pursuit can lead us into the same trap. Balance is the middle position and the one we need to aim to achieve.

As Krish Kandiah has expressed it:

A while back I found out that watching television was regularly taking up a massive four hours of my day. Radical action was needed. Sometimes I check my diary and find that I am out at work several evenings in a row. Radical action is needed. Sometimes church activities are taking up all my waking hours; radical action is needed. Work–life balance is more than a buzzword; it is walking the knife-edge between two of the devil's best-utilised traps: being idle or making an idol out of work.[14]

Lesson 2: Never tire of doing right
Paul encouraged his friends in Thessalonica:

As for you, brothers and sisters, never tire of doing what is right.[15]

We can be too easily influenced by our culture and its tastes. That is especially true in the area of leisure. Who would have believed just a few decades ago that we would describe leisure as an industry? But that is what it has become – a big money-spinner in most Western countries, creating thousands of jobs.

As with anything in life, however, we can become victims of excess, so we are warned regularly about the inherent dangers of eating and drinking too much. The same is true of leisure if it becomes nothing more than an excuse for over-indulging.

Perhaps, for us, *never tiring of doing what is right* may mean a different look at how we use our leisure time. We have more free time than our parents and grandparents thought possible. Holidays and weekends, budget airlines and getaway breaks have created seemingly endless opportunities to 'get away from it all'. But there needs to be a balance and, wearing my pastor's hat for a moment, local churches can't run on part-time members. It's impossible to build community if the same congregation doesn't meet for several weeks running. Believe me, I have been there, and what you end up with is not church, but a type of religious association with little sense of identity or mission.

So how do we find that balance of using leisure time in a more useful way? Instead of spending time on ourselves, how about using it as time for others? Turning leisure time into serving time can be – quite literally – life-changing. Let me share a few examples I know of personally.

I think of Sandra, who spends two weeks every summer as a care assistant at a holiday hotel for people with severe disabilities. This has become a highlight of her year and an opportunity to meet a whole group of new friends. She didn't need to fill her time, but some years ago she felt she wanted to use her generous holiday allowance to benefit others. She had no previous knowledge of working with people with disabilities, and confesses to having been quite scared at the prospect. But she has found that the experience has opened a new door of personal growth.

Then there is a family I know who have spent several Christmas Days cooking meals and organizing games for people who would otherwise be home alone. They have catered for several hundred people and brought much joy over the years by investing their leisure time in this way.

At a personal level, I recall the generosity of two friends named Liz and Ruth who, at different times, offered to act as honorary nannies to our children, providing us with the opportunity to have a few days away from the busy demands of local church life.

Then there are the church groups who take on work projects in other countries as an act of service. As I write this chapter, I can think of several in the past few months who have undertaken building and renovation projects in various parts of the world. The benefits of these short-term service projects are amazing – for those who serve as much as for those who are served.

If we open our eyes, examples and opportunities surround us.

Lesson 3: The power of example

Paul was able to point to his own example of hard work and discipline as the way a follower of Jesus should behave. Paul had studied under the famous Jewish Rabbi Gamaliel, and understood the power of personal example. The rabbis taught by having their pupils sit at their feet, and their lessons of theology and spirituality went beyond dry lectures. They shared life with their students.

This is one reason behind Paul's strong insistence on example. We live in a culture where mentoring and personal coaching have become standard practice in some areas of work life. The concept that we always have something new to learn, some skill to refine and develop, is not a foreign language.

I want to suggest, however, that this learning by example is something we would do well to harness and use proactively as a resource within the local church. How often do we ask those who seem to achieve balance in their life to share their experience? I often wonder if we should swap yet another Bible study for an evening on life skills such as managing teenagers, running a home, being a Christian entrepreneur, or finding time to be a lay reader, raise a family and hold down a job.

We need to relearn the power of example and use it to encourage a new generation of Christians to go further than we have done.

Key point
- **God wants us to be useful, not idle.**
- **We should never tire of doing what is right (which means using leisure time well).**
- **We need to remember the power of example (and use it to encourage a new generation).**

Making a difference

Emma works in a busy office. Some time ago, she began to pray seriously about how she could express her faith at work.

She had a surprising answer to her prayers.

One Friday she was working late to finish a report, and as she switched off the lights she looked around the open-plan office and saw stacks of dirty cups and saucers strewn across desks. She knew the contract cleaners flatly refused to wash them and would simply dust around the debris when they came in at the weekend.

Suddenly Emma saw her answer staring her in the face.

Not only does she stay to wash up the dirty cups regularly now, but she brings in fresh flowers too. By God's grace, she is making a difference in her office.

For further thought . . .

1. Is the temptation to laziness something you struggle with? How do you overcome it?

2. 'Never tire of doing right.' What are some of the right things you are doing – or might begin to do?

3. Do you agree that the power of example is the best teacher? Identify someone who has had that kind of influence on you and pinpoint the specific things that have impressed you.

5. LIKE A CANDLE IN THE WIND

In preparing to write this book, I decided to undertake some research into company mission statements. I wanted to discover how large organizations viewed what they stood for. Here is a selection of what I found:

We should set high standards and expect to be judged by them. The quality we aim for in all of our dealings is that of integrity.

Our first priority is integrity in our dealings as a financial services institution.

Integrity is never compromised. The conduct of our company worldwide must be pursued in a manner that is socially responsible and commands respect for its integrity and its positive contributions to society.

We are committed at all times to integrity and fairness.

All employees should seek to uphold and enhance the standing of the company by maintaining an unimpeachable standard in integrity in all their business relationships.

Our Companies insist on honesty and integrity in all aspects of the business.

We conduct our business with uncompromising integrity.

Our reputation for integrity is the foundation on which mutual trust between the company and its customers must be based.

Care must be taken in the selection of agents and consultants, who should be persons of the highest integrity.

You will have spotted the connecting word – *integrity*. We use it in the context of honesty and truthfulness, but it also conveys the idea of being whole or united. Integrity involves being integrated with no compartments hidden away or closed off. It is a very biblical concept, as holiness carries the parallel idea of wholeness. So go back through the statements above and substitute the word 'holiness' where 'integrity' appears. Suddenly the New Testament takes on a Monday-morning feel. Companies want integrity at the heart of their business and disciples of Jesus are called to have integrity at the heart of their lives. Which makes followers of Christ the people every company would want to employ.

One of the biggest challenges we face is to live consistently as a Christian.

Or does it?

Many of us admit that one of the biggest challenges we face is to live consistently as a Christian – and the workplace is one of the main arenas where that particular battle is waged.

There are occasions when we feel out on a limb and unsure of what we can do or how we should respond in a given situation. We desire consistency, but don't want to come across as wet. We see the need for a Christian voice in the workplace, but dislike the thought of becoming a megaphone. 'Like a candle in the wind' perhaps sums up how we sometimes feel at our most vulnerable.

Key point
For a follower of Christ, integrity is the goal for the whole of life – including the workplace.

In this chapter we shall consider three important areas in the world of work:

- Success
- Stress
- Strength.

To learn what Scripture has to say on these topics, we shall look at one of the most remarkable stories in the Old Testament – the story of Joseph.

Success at work

Joseph was one of twelve sons born to Jacob. They were part of the family line of Abraham and played a significant part in the unfolding story of the nation of Israel. The twelve sons became the clan heads of the twelve tribes of Israel and their names were embedded within the history of the Jews.

Joseph was born as the second youngest at a crucial time in Jacob's life. He became the apple of his father's eye, but Jacob didn't handle the situation with wisdom and honoured his son Joseph in a very special way by giving him a richly ornamented robe.[1] This was in a culture where normally the eldest was the honoured son, and this created jealousy within the family.

Joseph displayed the naivety of a teenager when he began to talk about his dreams. Although in time they were proved to be prophetically accurate, the timing of his revelations and the way in which he described them only fuelled the resentment against him. Joseph reached the point where his brothers hated him with a vengeance.[2] The story took a dramatic twist when he visited his brothers, who were tending the family flocks some distance from home. Their hatred of Joseph had reached boiling point and they decided to kill him and cover up the murder by claiming that he had been gored by a wild animal.

But one of them, Reuben, stood up for his younger brother and suggested, 'Look, instead of killing him, throw him in this well.' He said this to buy time, as his intention was to rescue Joseph, but he didn't have the courage to confront his brothers directly about their evil intentions.

Joseph was captured by his brothers, who changed their murderous plan and sold him to passing traders as a slave. They took his trademark robe, tore it and dipped it in the blood of an animal. They returned to their father with the story that they had found the bloodstained robe, but no trace of Joseph. Jacob was heartbroken at this terrible news and refused all attempts to comfort him.

Joseph was sold as a slave in Egypt and ended up in the home of a man named Potiphar, who was a senior military man in Pharaoh's household.

> The LORD was with Joseph and he prospered, and he lived in the house of his Egyptian master. When his master saw that the LORD was with him and that the LORD gave him success in everything he did, Joseph found favour in his eyes and he became his attendant. Potiphar put him in charge of his household, and he entrusted to his care everything he owned. From the time he put him in charge of his household and of all that he owned, the LORD blessed the household of

the Egyptian because of Joseph. The blessing of the LORD
was on everything Potiphar had, both in the house and in
the field. So he left in Joseph's care everything he had; with
Joseph in charge, he did not concern himself with anything
except the food he ate.[3]

If you carry responsibility, you will know it is a heavy load. If
you are in charge of other people, you will have experienced
the stress of managing not just their time but their problems
and expectations as well. So imagine the touch of heaven
Potiphar experienced when he realized that in this foreign
slave, Joseph, he had found an individual whom he could
trust. He could give his time and energy to other things
because, with Joseph running his household, he felt confident
that everything at home was in a safe pair of hands. Joseph
may have been a foreigner and a slave, but he possessed more
than a touch of class.

Several things stand out from this account.

Joseph got on with his life
Instead of being consumed by regret and the desire for
revenge, Joseph got on with his life. Homesickness and the
pain of rejection must have figured large in his emotional
response as he thought about his family, but he refused to
live as a victim. He was not trapped
in the downward spiral of self-
pity, but determined that he would
make the best of some awful
circumstances.

**Joseph refused
to live as
a victim.**

Not long ago, I sat with a woman
who blamed her sometimes bizarre behaviour on her
background. Because of what took place forty years ago, she
was asking people to make over-generous allowances for

her now. But this had become more of an excuse than an explanation. Grace helps us to grow, rather than stay locked in the past.

Joseph was a good worker

Joseph proved his worth to Potiphar over a period of time. Faithfulness in small things led to greater responsibility. He developed a reputation for reliability, which is something you don't achieve in five minutes. Track records like that take time, consistency and proof under pressure.

We are reminded that success in one project is not enough. Being a consistent and reliable worker is the goal to aim at. Small things (getting to work on time, putting in your full hours, delivering to deadlines, honesty and good relationships) make big reputations.

God was with Joseph

There is no greater accolade that can be given than this: God believes in you so much that he chooses to be with you. Every temptation to abandon his faith in the face of adversity was rejected by Joseph. He proved the truth of the promise:

> Those who honour me I will honour, but those who despise me will be disdained.[4]

How do we measure our success at work? There are various familiar ways such as appraisal, promotion, salary increases, commendations and the like. But the model of Joseph's life is a pattern that helps us to see how God measures success. And that is particularly helpful when we are short on rewards of the other kind.

Stress at work

There is much published research on stress in the workplace. One survey asked managers how their work affected the rest of life. The results make disturbing reading.

How Work Affects Life[5]

A sample group of managers reported:

87% – I have no time for other interests.
71% – My job is damaging my health.
86% – My work affects my relationship with my children.
79% – My work affects my relationship with my partner.
68% – My responsibilities reduce my productivity.

Another piece of academic work by a joint US/UK group reported on attitudes to work in the UK. The team reported the following points.

- Only one in three Britons enjoy their job.
- The UK was rated seventeenth in the International League Table of Job Satisfaction.
- The UK was bottom of all European nations tabled.
- The main pressures were longer hours, problems of commuting and job insecurity.
- Research shows this is a downward trend that has been continuing for several years.[6]

Not many would argue that the workplace is a stress-free zone. In the UK it is estimated that work-related stress is responsible for 6 million days of sick leave a year, with stress being linked to many minor and major illnesses.

The majority of us spend around 25% of our adult lives working. Work can provide us with structure, purpose, satisfaction, self-esteem and spending power, but it can also be a source of debilitating worry.[7]

Joseph faced a particular kind of stress in his working life – sexual harassment.[8]

Potiphar's wife became sexually attracted to Joseph and made numerous attempts to lure him into her bed. The Bible says that Joseph was a well-built and handsome young man and she was probably a lonely woman with her husband preoccupied with affairs of state. This was a recipe for a steamy affair. Joseph managed to keep the lady at bay with the use of some skilful avoidance tactics, but one particular day he found himself in the house alone with her. She grabbed his cloak and implored him for sex, but he ran out of the house, leaving his cloak behind.

Angry at being rejected, the woman made up a story of attempted rape using the abandoned cloak as evidence. Potiphar, furious at this breach of trust, had Joseph thrown into jail without trial – and little prospect of reprieve.

As we think about the topic of integrity in the workplace, Joseph's painful experience offers some principles worth pondering.

Joseph listened to his heart, not his hormones

In Western society we tend to live by our appetites. 'If it feels good, do it!' was the 1960s mantra that has become received wisdom. But appetite by nature is greedy, self-indulgent and a dangerous guide. Joseph used his brain and reasoned that he had responsibilities to his God, his boss, his boss's wife – and to himself. The Bible doesn't say if Potiphar's wife was beautiful, or whether Joseph felt attracted to her in any way. Those are superficial issues as far as the narrative is concerned. Joseph was caught up with his moral responsibilities rather than looking for a couple of hours of fun in the bedroom.

I have had some uncomfortable conversations in my life with men and women who have got caught up in an affair. As a pastor, I have been involved in helping them to pick up the pieces of a broken relationship and, believe me, it is a messy business. I have lost count of the times I have heard phrases such as 'I couldn't help myself', 'The attraction was overwhelming – I couldn't do anything about it', 'It just happened'. The common theme in all these excuses (for that is what they are) is that we are incapable of controlling ourselves. That is what happens when we listen to our hormones rather than our hearts. Joseph had a holy fear of God that we would do well to cultivate if we want to find true wisdom.[9]

Joseph held fast under pressure

The narrative contains a little phrase which is all too easy to pass over:

> And though she spoke to Joseph day after day, he refused to go to bed with her or even to be with her.[10]

We can't tell how long 'day after day' meant, but it conveys the idea that the woman kept up her seduction campaign for some considerable time. Joseph felt the pressure so much that he avoided being around as much as he could – which must have produced some difficulties as he was running the household. (I wonder if he had an assistant he could rely on?)

We all face different pressures in our lives.

We all face different pressures in our lives and some of us find them easier to handle than others. The pressure to conform to the surrounding culture is strong when we are at work and we need boundaries and safety valves in place. Boundaries are personal rules that we make about what we will and won't do. Safety valves are ways of releasing the steam when the pressure builds. If you are not sure how to go about finding your own set, ask someone whom you identify as a good role model how they have learned to live with pressure.

Joseph knew when to quit

On the day this sorry saga boiled over, Joseph found himself in a compromising situation, alone in the house with Potiphar's wife. As she made her move, Joseph took the only course open to him and ran out of the house. There are times when we just have to say 'no' in order to maintain our integrity. And there are times when that may involve leaving our job rather than compromising our beliefs.

Some time ago, the press in the UK carried a story that illustrates the point. Two Christian workers in a plant nursery on the Isle of Wight found themselves at the centre of a controversy involving The British Tomato Growers Association. The Association had embraced the ancient Chinese philosophy of *feng shui* in the belief that it would greatly increase yield and quality, and every nursery in membership was expected to follow suit. The two workers approached the management to object to this approach, but they could not reach agreement. So the two quit their jobs. They made it clear that they were being asked to compromise their beliefs and this was what lay at the heart of the matter. Reading the reports, I was struck by a comment made by one of the workers:

> I couldn't live a contradiction. By teaching Sunday School one day and the next going to work for a company that openly proclaims a godless creed. I couldn't be associated with it in any way or I would be seen as approving of it.[11]

These are not easy decisions to take and are not ones that we should rush into, but where integrity is at stake, it is worth it. As someone said, 'Integrity is like virginity. Once you've lost it, it's gone.'

Strength at work

This particular episode in Joseph's life sees him in jail with little prospect of release. His situation is as bad as it ever was. But things have an optimistic ring as the scene is set for a surprise ending:

> But while Joseph was there in the prison, the LORD was with him; he showed him kindness and granted him favour in the eyes of the prison warder. So the warder put Joseph in charge of all those held in the prison, and he was made responsible for all that was done there. The warder paid no attention to anything under Joseph's care, because the LORD was with Joseph and gave him success in whatever he did.[12]

You may have heard the phrase 'character will out', and it is certainly borne out in Joseph's story. The anonymous jail director identifies what Potiphar had already seen. Joseph had leadership qualities and organizational skills and was 100% reliable. This part of the prison was different from the rest – it was where the king's prisoners were held, suggesting perhaps that it was slightly better than a dank dungeon. But the narrator of the story wants us as readers to be in no doubt as to the source of Joseph's success. It was more than a case of raw talent; Joseph knew God's hand on his life. And that could be the subtitle to the whole of his story. With respect to Messrs Rice and Lloyd Webber, the amazing thing about Joseph was not his technicolour dreamcoat, but the God he worshipped.

The source of Joseph's strength at work was this relation-ship with the God of his fathers. The story continues with amazing twists and turns, until Joseph becomes prime minister of Egypt, having managed the nation through economic periods of boom and bust. His skills in running a large house and ordering a prison proved valuable in time. Unlike with some, the sweet smell of success did not turn his head and his faith was as rich and real in his finest hours as it was in the darkest ones.[13]

Jesus taught that you could always tell a tree by its fruit, and even a brief glance at Joseph's life reveals a rich harvest. He displayed:

- personal integrity under pressure;
- a willingness to forgive those who wronged him;
- a refusal to retreat into self-pity;
- an ability to make the best of every bad situation;
- strength of character that was obvious to others;
- sound judgment and wise speech.

There is an interesting reference to Joseph's suffering in one of the psalms, which gives a clue to the spiritual training God was putting him through.

> They bruised his feet with shackles,
>   his neck was put in irons,
> till what he foretold came to pass,
>   till the word of the LORD proved him true.[14]

Joseph had dreams as a young man that showed God's end purpose in his life, but to his family the very idea that they would bow down and give him honour was preposterous and undoubtedly ignited the fire of bitter resentment his brothers felt towards him. God's prophetic promise, however, was fulfilled only after the word had proved or tried him. Joseph's confinement was about refinement. He passed the proving process well and his adolescent dreams found fulfilment, in God's good time.[15]

Joseph's varied work roles were not particularly 'spiritual' and he was living (like Daniel) in a pagan nation. Yet he found strength from God for his daily responsibilities. We can find the same strength.

Integrity ran through Joseph's life like a rich seam of gold. David Pawson offers the following assessment:

> Joseph is unspoiled either by humiliation or honour. He is a man of total integrity and the only one so presented in the Old Testament. All the Old Testament characters are presented with their weaknesses as well as their strengths, but here is a man who only has strengths. There is only one other person in the Bible who is like this.[16]

We should not be intimidated by such an accolade; rather, we should be inspired.

Key point
The story of Joseph reminds us that we can know success, manage stress and discover strength in our working lives.

Pursuing excellence

One of the most famous landmarks of London is the statue of Eros in Piccadilly Circus. Few recall why the statue – which symbolizes love – was placed in the central London square. It was built in memory of Anthony Ashley Cooper, the seventh Earl of Shaftesbury (1801–85), who was a social philanthropist with some extraordinary achievements to his credit. He became a voice for the voiceless and a champion of those who found themselves marginalized. He used his skills as a parliamentarian to introduce massive social change that benefited thousands of people. He was a tireless Christian who wanted his faith in Jesus Christ to be worked out in his everyday world. For him, young children and women being forced to work in terrible conditions became an issue of faith; the proper care of those with mental illness became an issue of faith; provision of education for those who were at the bottom of the social scale became an issue of faith. Anthony Ashley Cooper had more than a Sunday-morning faith. He wanted to live an integrated life.

Next time you visit Piccadilly Circus, read the inscription at the foot of the statue of Eros. The words are from the pen of British prime minister William Ewart Gladstone, who paid a nation's tribute to the late earl:

> During a public life of half a century he devoted the influence of his station, the strong sympathies of his heart, and the great powers of his mind, to honouring God by serving his fellow-men, an example of his order, a blessing to this people, and a name to be by them ever gratefully remembered.

Truly, an example of a candle in the wind.

For further thought . . .

1. Can you think of recent examples, either at work or in the news, where a person's integrity has been noticeably clear or blatantly absent?

2. Reviewing Joseph's life story, what aspects of his character stand out most of all to you?

3. Can you identify specific areas in which you struggle to maintain integrity at work?

6. WHEN I'M SIXTY-FOUR

A manager found his authority increasingly challenged by staff and decided to underline who was in charge. He purchased a large, bright sign, which he hung on his office door. Emblazoned across it in red capitals were two words: *The Boss*.

When he returned from lunch, he found a small Post-it® note stuck to the sign that read: 'While you were at lunch your wife phoned. She asks if you could let her have her sign back, please!'

One of the things that we have underlined so far in this book is that, for a Christian, the issue about 'the Boss' is very clear. It does not matter who we are or what we do, whether we are in paid employment or not: if we are a child of God, then part of being a disciple is recognizing the lordship of Jesus.

The theme of this chapter is borrowed from the famous song by Lennon and McCartney that poignantly asks whether young love can last through a lifetime and into old age. 'Will you still need me,' the song asks, 'when I'm sixty-four?'

The message of the song is simple: life changes and we change with it. This is especially true within the world of work.

This chapter will have something to say about retirement, but it goes wider than that. It is about how we find God in those changing periods we all face in life. It may be a change of job, or even a switch of career path. Or it may be the challenge of going back to work after a period, or moving from part-time to full-time employment. We are looking at how we can manage such changes with confidence and faith.

Time for everything

Gail's life has been a story of change. She left school, joined the civil service and eventually passed a promotion exam and was moved to a new posting in London, far away from the north-country town where she had grown up. She was happy in the nation's capital, got stuck into her job and made many new friends. She also found a new faith and a husband, Mark. Five years after her move to the south of England, they married and bought a flat an hour's commuting distance from work.

Mark was promoted in his company and the increased salary meant they could afford a small maisonette in Essex. The daily commute was longer, but they appreciated the chance to buy a house that they could gradually turn into a home. Then Gail fell pregnant and life took another turn. Their first child, Chris, was a total joy to them both.

Fast-forward ten years. Gail and Mark have three children, and have moved to a larger house in the same town. Gail has not returned to full-time work, but is busily involved in her local Anglican church. She helps in the parish office three mornings a week, which fits neatly with taking and collecting the children from school. Mark's job has changed and he works for a company with branches across Europe, which means that most weeks he is away travelling for two or three nights.

Fast-forward another ten years. Gail is back in full-time employment in the local town hall. Chris is at university and their two girls look set on tertiary education as well. For sheer economic reasons, Gail realizes that she has to work to give the extra financial support her children need through their university studies. Returning to full-time work has been a major challenge for Gail. First there was the confidence hurdle – twenty years on, so much has changed. Then there was the new juggling act to be perfected – running the home, attending to the needs of three very different young people with GCSEs, A levels and university applications to contend with (not to mention hormones and testosterone).

Gail and Mark have not had the easiest time in their marriage for the past few years. Quality time seems to be reserved for holidays and an odd evening out for a birthday or anniversary. A large German firm bought out Mark's company two years ago and his position looks more tenuous by the day. The strain of a new regime and a new business model has been enormous and Mark has become weighed down under the pressure of it all. He has been scouring the employment ads for months in the hope of finding something that will prove less stressful – but nothing has emerged.

Their church suffered a messy split a few years ago when a significant number of younger members started a new, independent congregation. It was a move surrounded with bad feeling and recrimination. Out of loyalty to the vicar, Gail insisted that they stay on to support St Mary's through what she felt sure was no more than a passing phase. But the church has not yet recovered and the vicar moved on in the aftermath of the split. The new vicar is a woman and Mark struggles with her whole approach, while Gail sees her as a gifted and resourceful pastor who has much to offer a wounded congregation. As a result, church – which was once a haven – has become a source of tension, not least between Mark and Gail themselves.

A twenty-five-year whirlwind tour of Gail Walker's life reveals just a few of the changes she has had to negotiate. And there are more to come, with ageing parents, children deciding to live with their partner rather than get married, and Mark opting for early retirement on a far from adequate pension.

For the Gails and the Marks, the familiar poem in the book of Ecclesiastes has wise words to offer:

There is a time for everything,
and a season for every activity under heaven.[1]

We are called to worship one who is a God for all seasons. He is able to teach, encourage, guide, lead and provide, whatever is going on around and within. The famous 'shepherd psalm' speaks of his goodness and love pursuing us all the days of our lives – not just the ones when the sun shines.[2]

> Navigating change requires some fixed points that keep us on track.

Navigating change requires some fixed points that keep us on track. I want to suggest four out of several we can find within Scripture. I call them 'principles', because that is what they are.

Principle 1: God has something for us to do in every season
Most of us enjoy routine because the familiar is safe. We like to know where we are and what we will be doing. When change threatens, we feel insecure and afraid that what is coming will not be as good as what has been before. Anyone involved in what is called the management of change will recognize the importance of reassuring people that change will produce benefits.

Change is part of life and we need to learn the skill of adjustment.

A friend recently retired and the company he worked for arranged for him to go on a pre-retirement course. It was a well-organized event that looked at issues such as money, health, hobbies and using time to serve the wider community.

Whoever designed the course deserved an award, because my friend came home fired with enthusiasm for what he saw as a new chapter in his life.

I thought hard about his response and realized that what had made him positive was the signal that there was purpose in what lay ahead. He and his wife had been alerted to the future change and were better prepared to negotiate the adjustments that would be involved.

As we face change, it is good to ask God for the ability to discover purpose in the new chapter he has opened for us. Who are the people with whom we can build relationships? What is the value I can bring to this new period in my life? How can I use my God-given skills to the full in this situation? Why has God put me here? These are some of the questions we need to address as we set out to discover God's will in the changing seasons of life. Earlier we looked at the word 'vocation' and saw that it refers to a sense of calling. The challenge is to sense God's call in the change and to see it as an exciting possibility rather than a negative threat.

It is also healthy to list the things we are worried about, rather than let them fester under the surface. I recently had a meal with a university student who was applying for a job, his first. As we talked, Jon shared three or four worries he had about the interview process, plus the challenge of which jobs to apply for. His ability to identify these things put him in a stronger position to face them. I ended our meal by reminding him of his first few weeks at university, when he faced a similar change. He had seen many answers to prayer over those three years and had made some great friends. He had found God's grace many times in that season of change and had every reason to trust that he would find the same to be true in the big unknown that lay ahead.

Principle 2: *None of us need live feeling that we're on the scrapheap*

Living in another culture for a time helps you to look at your own values with different eyes.

I spent several months working in India some years ago and learned some valuable lessons. For one thing, very few items were totally discarded. There was always someone who could repair and reuse things. This stood in contrast to our own culture, where we accept that things have a limited lifespan. How many times have we heard the words, 'It's cheaper to buy a new one than have this repaired'?

Part of the pressure of a throwaway culture is that we apply the same principle to people. Once you hit a certain age you become unemployable, not because you can't do the job, but because the company no longer employs people beyond that age threshold.

For example, there was Frank, in his mid-fifties, who founded a company and spent twenty years building the business with energy and drive. He sold it on the understanding that he would remain on the board, but within a few months he was told by the new owner, 'Thanks, but we don't need you any more. Your services are surplus to requirements.'

Or take Becky, whose school merged with another and didn't need two heads of department. They opted for the younger candidate and suggested that Becky should see this as a chance for early retirement.

Then there is Richard, who lost his job in banking two years ago and has tried every door, only to find it locked. I asked if he struggled with the rejection letters and he told me they were not as bad as the people who promised to contact him and never bothered.

There are complicated factors in all these cases, but behind the arguments are three people who have skills and talents to offer. They are full of life experience and are willing to work hard, yet no-one, it seems, places any value on them. That is both demoralizing and disheartening. And for all three it throws up some big faith issues as well.

Tony Blair served as the British prime minister for a decade and was in office at the turn of the millennium. Two comments he made offer a penetrating insight into the spiritual emptiness of British society:

> Britain has never been more affluent and has never been so unhappy.[3]

Earlier, in a Labour Party document, he had written:

> We enjoy a thousand material advantages over any previous generation and yet we suffer a depth of insecurity and spiritual doubt that they never did.

Note that this was the prime minister, not the archbishop of Canterbury, or someone else we would expect to offer that kind of assessment. He was saying that we have never had so much, but we have never been so empty. We have never had so much to live *with* and yet so little to live *for*. Perhaps that malaise is seen most clearly in the way we devalue people and make the bottom line one of financial profit.

The Bible teaches that every human being has an intrinsic value, because we are made in the image of God. Rather than shrugging our shoulders and accepting 'that's the way things are', the challenge is to recover that God-given sense of worth and value. We may have lost a job title and the salary that goes with it, but we need not lose our sense of dignity and self-respect.

If we open our eyes, there are opportunities everywhere to utilize our skills and prove our value. Local schools need volunteers to listen to children read, voluntary organizations are always looking for extra hands and in any community there are people who need and appreciate help of all kinds. And for those with entrepreneurial skills, the possibilities are limitless. Use your imagination and creative skills. Find the gaps and plug them!

Debra Searle is a remarkable woman who is a motivational speaker of the highest quality. In her best-selling book *The Journey*,[4] she tells the story of how she came to row the Atlantic Ocean alone after her husband, Andrew, was unable to continue the race. Over three months she rowed 3,000 gruelling miles for twelve hours a day and eventually made land, having completed the challenge alone.

In front of her as she rowed was a slogan that became her daily inspiration:

Choose Your Attitude.

I have heard her speak to audiences on this theme. She embodies this principle that none of us need live feeling that we're on the scrapheap. We can choose our attitude as we face each new day. It can be anger, bitterness, indignation or a simmering desire to hit back. Or we can choose forgiveness, hope, the desire for a new challenge. Then we have a chance to find joy at the prospect of a whole new chapter about to begin.

Principle 3: Whatever you do, do it with all your might
This comes straight out of the pages of the Old Testament, from the book of Ecclesiastes to which we referred earlier.

Whatever your hand finds to do, do it with all your might, for in the grave, where you are going, there is neither working nor planning nor knowledge nor wisdom.[5]

As the Latin motto says, *carpe diem* – 'seize the day'. Make the most of what you have been given and use every opportunity that comes your way. I think that for a person with a living, personal faith this is even more important. If we believe that our very lives are a gift on trust, then that is greater motivation to find usefulness. All my life, as I have observed people and the outcome of their lives, I have noticed that the most contented are the ones whose lives are characterized by generosity and serving others. Equally I have noticed that the more self-centred an individual is, the greater is that person's sense of dissatisfaction.

We come closest to the Servant King as we ourselves learn to stoop and serve.

It was my privilege to meet Mother Teresa of Calcutta on two occasions. She was a woman small of stature yet big of soul. One phrase from our conversations stands out: 'If you want to get close to Jesus, work with poor people. You find him with the poor.' Her life of self-sacrifice and service to others had taught her a profound lesson of faith. We come closest to the Servant King as we ourselves learn to stoop and serve.

Some years ago, *Time* magazine ran an article on Mother Teresa and quoted her as saying, 'I do not know how others see me. I see myself as a little pencil in the hand of God.'

Whatever our job, that seems a good pattern to follow.

Principle 4: Seek first God's kingdom

There are some familiar words of Jesus contained in what we call the Sermon on the Mount, which deal with the issue of worry. Many have read these words and found them a great antidote to the fear that can often hang over us like a dark cloud. Jesus pointed to the birds and flowers, described how God as Creator provides for them and urged us not to be consumed with worry.[6]

Sandwiched in the middle of these words of assurance that urge us not to worry, but to trust God instead, comes a statement that we must not miss:

> But seek first his kingdom and his righteousness, and all these things will be given to you as well.[7]

It is one of those statements that we can easily read out of context and by so doing miss the meaning. Jesus is talking about how we can easily become preoccupied with things like money, clothes and food, to the extent that we neglect to put our trust fully in God. Times of change can create feelings of insecurity and cause us to be consumed by anxious thoughts. By consciously choosing to seek God's kingdom first, we can find ourselves released from worry about what the future may or may not bring.

Seeking God's kingdom first is not a cliché, but is seen in the choices we make. For instance:

- committing our future to God through our prayers;
- asking God to sift our motives so that our decisions are uncluttered;
- looking for ways in which we can express our trust in and dependence on God;

- identifying those things we struggle with in the change process;
- seeking to grow in our faith through this experience.

Whatever changes come our way during the course of our working life, we need not face them on our own. Perhaps that is the greatest reassurance of them all: we are not alone.

Key point
We can find hope and fulfilment in the changing seasons as we recognize that:
- **God has something for us to do in every season;**
- **none of us need live feeling that we're on the scrapheap;**
- **whatever we do, we should do it with all our might;**
- **it is important to seek first God's kingdom.**

A few days ago I received an e-mail from friends who have been visiting several African countries and looking at various projects offering help to those suffering through HIV / Aids. They wrote of the dedication and skill of those they had met, many of whom are professionals in medicine offering their skills to combat this modern scourge. But one pair of Christians left an indelible impression on my friends. They were not doctors, but an ordinary couple who found God in a changing season. Let me quote from part of the e-mail.

There are so many stories, but I will tell just one. We met this elderly Canadian couple, who we had seen doing office work around the base. So, we sat and had a cup of tea with them. They told us their retirement had been all planned out for years. Recreational Vehicle purchased, time-share holiday home bought – all the good things planned. Then the Lord got a hold of their hearts and led them to Uganda. Now they handle all the accounts for the base and – in addition – have organized and built a primary school for kids too poor to travel to the next region to be educated. They have 250 kids attending and it's growing! They employ 17 local Ugandans and each family contributes something to the running of the school but no one is turned away if they can't pay. The amazing thing is that everyone has been able to pay something and there is such a sense of ownership in the community. As they sat and shared their story I was overcome with emotion and joy. What a rewarding retirement for this loving couple!

The Lord has a purpose for every season of life.

I have a hunch that it was no coincidence that the e-mail arrived as I sat down to write this chapter. The Lord has a purpose for every season of life and he invites us to seek his will and find his plan as the changes come.

For further thought . . .

1. Think back to some of the periods of change in your life. How have you dealt with them? Can you identify some good things that have come from the experience?

2. Recalling Debra Searle's inspirational motto, 'Choose Your Attitude', how could this help you to navigate change successfully?

3. Which of the four principles outlined in this chapter do you find the most applicable in your present circumstances?

7. WITH A LITTLE HELP FROM MY FRIENDS

Most of us have discovered that work can, at times, be more frustrating than fulfilling. But some days it can be plain bizarre. Here are a few true snapshots from other people's working days.

- A librarian is approached by an elderly lady clutching a book. 'Excuse me,' she asks the bemused librarian, 'can you tell me if I have read this one?'
- A harassed mum collects four children on the school run and drops one at a music lesson, one at football practice and one at a friend's birthday party. She braves the rush-hour traffic and manages to arrive at the dentist with seconds to spare. She ushers the fourth into the surgery. The dentist examines the child's open mouth and declares, 'This child doesn't need a filling.' The mum stares at the child silently before leaping to her feet with the cry, 'Oh no . . . I've brought the wrong one!'
- The staff at a McDonald's restaurant decide to observe Remembrance Day on 11 November. As 11 a.m. approaches they respectfully invite customers to join in the one-minute silence. The time passes and the restaurant returns to normal business – only to be stormed by armed policemen a few minutes later. A well-meaning passer-by had seen staff and customers standing still and had called the police, saying they thought an armed robbery was taking place.
- A man was due to make an important presentation to the senior managers of his company. He had spent months on the project and now the big day had arrived.

His wife offered to press the trousers of his best suit as he put the final papers into his briefcase. He rushed down the stairs, neatly attired in jacket and tie, gave his wife a hasty kiss and made for the front door. 'Do you think you're going to need these?' asked his wife, holding up his freshly pressed trousers.

- A customer care supervisor in a mail-order company took a call from an irate customer. The caller complained that she had been sent a blue jumper instead of a white one. The supervisor checked the original order form and reported, 'You ordered the jumper in cornflower – and that's blue.' 'No it's not,' retorted the customer. 'I've just checked in the larder and my cornflour is white!'

Whatever shape our work may take, and whether it is paid or voluntary, most of us discover that we can have good days as well as the other kind.

With a little help from my friends

It is easy to feel isolated in the world of work. Yet church is sometimes the last place where we feel we can turn for help.

> **If we can't share work pressures within the family of God, things have gone seriously wrong.**

As one friend candidly explained, 'A few years back, when I was facing incredible pressure at work, I didn't know where to turn for help. In the end it was my non-Christian colleagues who proved to be the best help. No-one in my church could understand or help with what I faced.'

Here's my question: Should it be like that? If we can't share work pressures within the family of God, things have gone seriously wrong. If true *koinonia* (the Greek word that we translate into English as 'fellowship') is to be an experience rather than a theory, then surely the real stuff we battle with in life must surface within our relationships at church – and in that context we should be able to find support. Families that function well seem to do so on the basis of some kind of solidarity: we're in this together. And if local church is about building a community of believing people, then we need to relate together and support each other, especially in the tough times.

A friend recently took up the sport of bowls and told me how he felt welcomed and accepted within his club in a matter of weeks. He made new friends and discovered lots of things about their families and jobs in a short space of time. He told me, with a certain sense of puzzlement, 'I have not known that kind of openness and friendship after a lifetime of attending church.'

As a pastor, and someone who has been a leader in local churches, I confess to a huge sense of failure and responsibility when faced with comments like that. Whatever else we are seeking to achieve through our church programmes, if we are not building genuine community, then we are failing to express what it means to be the body of Christ in the twenty-first century.

Key point
To build a true sense of community we need to share what is happening in our lives, including our work.

In this chapter I want to explore some ways in which we can build the kind of open friendships within a congregation where we can share our lives and find mutual support.

Being willing to share – and to listen

Perhaps one of the first steps we can take is learning to create opportunities to share some of the important things happening in our working lives.

Equally important is a willingness to listen to each other. If we do not send a message that we are interested in the people around us and in what is happening in their lives, it is no wonder that things get buried and left unsaid.

A worse scenario still is when someone shares honestly, but the matter is not attended to properly.

Take the housegroup run by George and Heather as an example. They can gather anything up to ten people on a Tuesday evening and the group is a good cross section of ages represented in their church. All the housegroups at the Community Church follow the same study programme and at the moment they are working through Paul's letter to the Galatian churches.

Tonight is the final study based on Galatians 6, and it is led by George who faithfully follows the study guide provided by the church. After a short explanation of the passage, George announces that it's time for discussion and reads the first of several questions for the group to consider:

> Paul encourages the Galatians to 'carry each other's burdens, and in this way you will fulfil the law of Christ' (v. 2). What does that mean today for your group?

There follows some discussion about the need to visit those who are housebound, and the lack of helpers at the Saturday youth club.

George seems keen to wind things up. It's 9.25 and time for coffee. 'Anyone else?' he queries, in the manner of a pub landlord calling last orders.

Mel is the newest member of the group and has only been attending for three months. She was part of an Alpha group and then started to attend church regularly – where she was welcomed with open arms. She is a single woman in her late twenties who works for an architect's practice in the town. Mel starts hesitantly. 'I'm not sure if this counts, but can we mention if the burden is to do with work stuff?'

The group is silent until George jumps in. 'I think, Mel, it covers everything – work, home, whatever. Just share your burden.'

Mel clears her throat. 'Well, it's a bit awkward. But, as some of you know, I'm working on the new marina project some miles from here. My boss, Andy, is the project leader and we're spending several days each month on site. We always stay in the same hotel and after dinner share a few drinks and, well, I don't know how to put this, but Andy has been coming on strong to me and I'm not sure how to deal with it.'

George, who (bless him) had a sheltered upbringing, enquires, 'Mel, what exactly does "coming on strong" mean these days?' He pauses, hoping the rest of the group will notice his warm, pastoral concern.

'He wants me to sleep with him,' Mel replies. 'But, judging from what he has told me, I don't think I'll get much sleep!'

The room goes deathly quiet. Heather leaps to the rescue with her 'hands up for coffee' routine and Tom intervenes on behalf of poor, speechless George. 'Mel, that's a question for the vicar, I feel. Bit beyond the remit of homegroup, I think. Tough situation, and I'm sure we wish you well, but I'm not sure it would be helpful for a group discussion.'

Time for coffee and real fellowship to begin.

The topic was never raised again. Not surprisingly, Mel stopped attending homegroup shortly after. And it was not long before she stopped attending church. She embarked on a brief affair with Andy and he ended up leaving his wife and three children to move into Mel's apartment. But within a year it was all over: Andy back home for another try, Mel working with a new firm in Newcastle and not bothering with church any more.

These were nice, well-meaning people – but without a clue about the real world.

Bearing each other's burdens? Not a chance.

A different kind of church culture

How can we build the kind of local churches where people like Mel find real support?

> **We can become agents for change.**

There are steps we can take as individuals that can begin to create a different kind of church culture. Rather than waiting for someone else to take the initiative, we can become agents for change. Let me suggest three fairly straight-forward ideas.

1. Be more open about life at work

The way to remove the invisible barrier caused by silence is to start talking. Make a conscious decision to talk about what goes on in your life when you are not attending a church event. If work is good, bad or just mundane and normal, let people know. If you don't have a paid job, but your life is filled with caring for children or a sick relative, then share what makes up your day.

We have just received a prayer letter from some friends studying at theological college. The most important prayer topic is for their young son, who is struggling to adapt to a new school and is exhibiting signs of a potentially serious condition. They didn't need to share that for prayer; they could have written a letter filled with fluffy clichés. But they chose to be real – and as a result will receive some real prayer support. Our friendship will go deeper too. If they had not been willing to share, we would have felt at a greater distance from them.

2. Find a friend

At the time of writing, I have a prayer partner who has helped me through one of the toughest years of my life. Nigel and I have been meeting for a couple of years and we have a fixed routine that works well. Close to my home is a man-made lake about two miles in circumference. We meet at 7.00 a.m. whatever the weather or season and we walk two brisk circuits. On the first lap we talk and catch up with family, work and following Jesus. The second lap is taken up with prayer for one another and the issues we face. In recent months, when things have been especially tough for me, we have put in three and on one occasion four circuits of the lake.

I would not have survived these past months without Nigel's prayer support. I think he would say the same, as he has undertaken a major change of direction in his career in the past twelve months.

No-one asked us to meet like this. We found each other because we saw the need.

> **We always find time for the things we consider important.**

All it needs is for someone to take the initiative. Two friends began a similar prayer partnership that has given birth to an informal organization for men. Based on their own experience of the value of building relationships that prize reality, accountability and spiritual growth, they are encouraging similar groups for men to be developed across the country.[1]

The battle most of us face is with time. There is simply not enough of it. If we had more time, there are lots of good things we would achieve. The truth is, however, that we always find time for the things we consider important.

So go on, make the time and find one or more friends with whom you can be real and pray.

3. Get your homegroup to get real

Many churches have homegroups of one sort or another. I have attended and led several with varying degrees of success. I am well aware that they can be good, bad, or in some cases downright ugly. Adrian Plass has done the worldwide church a great service by reminding us just how silly we followers of Jesus can be at times. Homegroups can, on occasions, be an aquarium of collective silliness that passes any kind of understanding. Even the angels are puzzled.

My suggestion is simply that, if you attend a homegroup, you arrange an evening when those present answer three questions:

1. What do you do in real life?
2. What things do you enjoy?
3. What things do you find hard?

It's not rocket science, but it will take your group to a new level. Try it and see.

Key point
Some ways in which we can create a different church culture include becoming more open about needs at work, forming prayer partnerships and encouraging housegroups to discover more about what their members do when not attending a church event.

For those who lead

You may be a leader of a local church wondering how you can create the kind of open community where people can share at a deeper level some of the things they struggle with in their working week. I want to put forward several practical suggestions born out of my own experience.

Teach a series of sermons on workplace theology

In the introduction to this book I explained something of my own journey in this regard. I can only encourage you to examine what the Bible says about work and see how this might have an impact on your teaching.

In addition I would encourage you to give opportunity to other people to preach and teach on the subject. Experience suggests that people in the marketplace communicate best to others in the marketplace. If you are planning a teaching series, then include a few people who can reflect on biblical truth from the perspective of their own working lives.

Create opportunities for people to share work pressures

Pastoral care needs to be both proactive and reactive. Most of the time we are trapped in reactive mode, responding to the myriad of crises that make up local church life.

Proactive care adopts a different stance and says, in effect, 'What can we do to help you move forward in your faith?' In one church where I served, we experimented with what became known as 'Pastoral Clinics' where different members of the church staff made themselves available to see people on set days during the week. Something I noticed early on was how a significant number of those who called in to see me wanted to talk about issues at work. Sometimes it was to seek prayer and advice about a job change, or maybe to share a particular difficulty they were facing. It helped me as a pastor to get a glimpse of people beyond a Sunday service and taught me a simple but profoundly important lesson about asking the question from time to time, 'How are things going at work?'

Encourage people to share prayer needs about their work

Earlier I referred to a prayer project that we ran alongside the teaching series on God and the workplace. Many churches offer prayer ministry and a growing number have teams of people trained in how to do this effectively.

We ran the project on the basis of confidentiality. Prayer cards were printed that read as follows:

> **God in my Workplace**
> I would like to request prayer this week for:
>
> I commit myself to pray daily for this request and would ask the prayer team to join me.

A box was placed near the platform and people were encouraged to drop their completed cards in it. As mentioned, we had a wide-ranging series of requests and some positive feedback about answers to the prayers that were offered.

We learned some valuable lessons through the project. First, that people were looking for someone to tell about work pressures. Second, that because we encouraged them to pray for their own particular request, people discovered (some told me for the first time) that prayer for work-related problems was a good thing. Third, as always happens when we see prayers answered, people got a faith lift. Fourth, I was reminded that teaching needs to be earthed and not left floating.

Organize some special interest group breakfasts

In one church where we served for twelve years, we organized a series of breakfasts for various occupational groups in the church. 'People in education', 'people in health care' and 'people in business' featured in the first three such gatherings.

We met in a neutral venue and after a breakfast and welcome from one of the ministers we invited a member of the church who worked in that particular sphere to speak. For those working in education we chose a retired head teacher with thirty-plus years of teaching experience; for medical workers it was a consultant surgeon who had come to the UK from the developing world to complete his training; and for those in business we invited a local business entrepreneur to give his perspective as a Christian on the world of work. Those who spoke were invited to talk about living out their Christian faith in their careers and to give some helpful examples (including mistakes) with which those present could identify.

Following each of the talks we invited people on their small tables to talk about the pluses and minuses of their jobs. Most of us find it easier to talk within a small group and there was a buzz of conversation as people discussed what they liked about their work and those things they struggled with. The breakfast concluded with an opportunity for people to pray together over situations they faced.

One encouraging by-product of the breakfasts was the series of relationships that were formed, with people promising to pray for one another and keep in touch over various issues that were raised. As church leaders we were reminded how, in a large congregation, people may not know what someone does for a living. Our targeted breakfasts helped people identify others in the same field of work and helped develop some wider support networks.

As a pastor I discovered that we were 'scratching where people itched' and responding to a felt need in the congregation that went beyond the usual remit of Sunday services. I also found it helpful to listen hard to what was shared, as it gave me the chance to understand some of the things people struggled with in their 9–5 world. The late Dr Martyn Lloyd-Jones often quoted the advice of the French clinician Laennec (who invented the stethoscope): 'Listen to your patient! He is giving you the diagnosis!' That is wise advice for any preacher who wants to connect.

Consider running a workplace workshop
This involves drawing together a group of Christians who have a proven track record in the world of work and inviting them to share their experience. Most congregations have people who have much to share, but rarely get the opportunity. They have banks of knowledge and experience that could be a help to others who are wanting to live out their faith in the workplace.

This kind of gathering usually works best around a meal that can provide a natural setting for questions and discussion.

Key point
It is vital for those who lead local congregations to find creative ways to blend the world of work and the world of local church.

A journey of a thousand miles
I know enough about running a local church to recognize that few leaders sit around wondering how to fill their week. The ideas shared in this chapter are no more than suggestions of how we can start to break down the barrier between secular

and sacred that holds us back from celebrating an integrated faith embracing the whole of life.

These ideas come from my own experience, and yours may be different. The important thing is that we find our own way to create communities where work and life outside the church programme get more than a passing glance.

In the words of the Chinese proverb, 'A journey of a thousand miles begins with a single step.'

For further thought . . .

1. If you were attending George's and Heather's housegroup, how would you have responded to Mel's dilemma about her boss coming on strong?

2. Does your local church have a good sense of community? Think of some practical ways in which this could be developed.

3. Review the suggestions mentioned in this chapter. How would they work in your church? Can you think of other ideas to help break down the secular/sacred barrier?

8. MILKING COWS FOR JESUS?

I conducted a wedding for a young couple twenty years or so ago. They were head over heels in love and on the day of the wedding they made an attractive pair as friends and family joined in a large celebration. The husband – I'll call him Brian – possessed extraordinary gifts for a man of his age. He was a natural entrepreneur, at ease with people of all backgrounds, and he had oceans of raw energy. Here was the proverbial man who could sell ice at the North Pole. He made no secret of his ambition to be a millionaire before he was forty. Heather was different. She wanted a nice home, but was not bothered with amassing a fortune. For her, friendships, family and the ability to enjoy life were priorities.

It didn't take long for that clash of priorities to sound dissonant chords in the relationship. As the years went by, and three children later, the noise got louder and louder. Too loud to last, in fact.

I bumped into Heather a few months ago and she told the sad story of two people who set out in Christian marriage with good intentions, but crashed and burned *en route*. Broken dreams, broken promises and some very broken people make up a messy aftermath. As Paul warned Timothy, it is possible to wander away from the faith and pierce yourself and others around you with many griefs, and all for the love of money.

We can chase after the wrong things in our work. Our marriages will be affected – and much else besides.

Wealth
One of the wrong things we can chase after in our work is money.

I am always curious about new ways of expressing things. Not long ago we talked about 'savings plans', which sounded very dull, but then we were introduced to the world of 'wealth management' and suddenly the products sounded sexy. 'Savings' conjures up pictures of piggy banks and long queues at the bank, but mention 'wealth' and you can smell the sun oil and hear the waves gently lapping against the hull of your yacht.

The Bible has much to say about money and it is not all bad news.

Take, for example, a passage from the Old Testament that probably gives the theological foundations for harvest festivals. Through Moses, Yahweh urged the nation of Israel not to forget their God who delivered them from the slavery of Egypt, led them through a wilderness for forty years and gave them a land full of good things to enjoy. Recognizing the danger that always lurks when life is no longer a struggle and the good times are really rolling, God adds this note of warning:

> You may say to yourself, 'My power and the strength
> of my hands have produced this wealth for me.' But
> remember the LORD your God, for it is he who gives
> you the ability to produce wealth and so confirms his
> covenant, which he swore to your forefathers, as it
> is today.[1]

The ability to create wealth is a God-given gift. Understanding that can liberate those who have special skills at making money yet may struggle with feelings of guilt. Wealth creation is a vital part of the economic landscape and communities need those who can do it well and with integrity.

A second example comes from the New Testament and ranks as one of the most misquoted verses in the Bible. See if you can spot where the misquote usually occurs:

> But godliness with contentment is great gain. For we brought nothing into the world, and we can take nothing out of it. But if we have food and clothing, we will be content with that. Those who want to get rich fall into temptation and a trap and into many foolish and harmful desires that plunge people into ruin and destruction. For the love of money is a root of all kinds of evil. Some people, eager for money, have wandered from the faith and pierced themselves with many griefs.[2]

The usual mistake is to say, 'Money is the root of all evil' – which it isn't! Money is neutral and can be used to build a hospital or make a nuclear warhead. It is the hands that control it that make the choice of how it is used. Paul, who wrote these words to a young pastor, is not making a value judgment about money in itself, but he is warning that it can be an intoxicating influence. What lies at the root of all kinds of evil is the *love* of money. Inner-city drug gangs, board-room battles, organized crime, corporate fraud scandals and more besides can all be traced to a common root, the love of money.

Like many other scriptures, these two passages need to be held in balance as they teach parallel truths. The ability to create wealth is God-given, but beware of loving money so much that it destroys you.

Key point
The ability to create wealth comes from God, but making wealth our god can only lead to pain.

The book of Ecclesiastes warns against some other potent temptations facing the worker.

Meaning

The book of Ecclesiastes has traditionally been understood as the work of King Solomon, whose wisdom and wealth were legendary. But it is probable that the work is from a later period and from an author who uses aspects of Solomon's life as illustrations to reinforce his point.[3] The writer takes a long, hard, honest look at life – including the world of work. The book is basically a big sermon and the word 'Ecclesiastes' can be translated as 'The Preacher'.[4] And the preacher has a text, which he announces at the beginning of his sermon:

> 'Meaningless! Meaningless!'
>   says the Teacher.
> 'Utterly meaningless! Everything is meaningless.'[5]

The writer is not simply suffering from a bad case of the blues, but is making a stark point: life without God is ultimately meaningless. Richard Dawkins may sell a lot of books and build an impressive following, but the verdict of the Bible is that his well-travelled route is a cul-de-sac. The preacher illustrates his uncomfortable conclusion from real-life experience. He lists the things he pursued in the vain hope that the answer to a fulfilled life lay hidden within them:

- wisdom and knowledge;[6]
- pleasure;[7]
- projects;[8]
- money and possessions;[9]
- sex and relationships.[10]

I denied myself nothing my eyes desired;
　　I refused my heart no pleasure.
My heart took delight in all my work,
　　and this was the reward for all my labour.
Yet when I surveyed all that my hands had done
　　and what I had toiled to achieve,
everything was meaningless, a chasing after the wind;
　　nothing was gained under the sun.[11]

Included in the writer's search for meaning is the world of work. He paints two contrasting pictures of work without God and work with God.

Work without God

Putting it bluntly, according to the Preacher, work without God is a pain:

So I hated life, because all the work that is done under the sun was grievous to me. All of it is meaningless, a chasing after the wind.[12]

He suggests three outcomes that drove him to this conclusion.

1. You can't take wealth with you when you die

I hated all the things I had toiled for under the sun, because I must leave them to the one who comes after me.[13]

As the Spanish proverb expresses it, 'There are no pockets in a shroud.' You can spend your working life amassing the cash, only to leave it all behind when you make the final journey from this life to the next.

2. You leave to somebody else what you've worked so hard to gain

The writer struggled with the thought that all the fruit of his hard work might not be appreciated or used well by the ones who inherited it:

> And who knows whether that person will be wise or foolish? Yet my heir will have control over all the work into which I have poured my effort and skill under the sun.[14]

3. It's not worth all the hassle

As depressing as it may sound, the preacher of this honest message concludes that work without a God-dimension is empty of meaning:

> What do people get for all the toil and anxious striving with which they labour under the sun? All their days their work is pain and grief; even at night their minds do not rest. This too is meaningless.[15]

Reading this, I find I want to heckle the Preacher midway through his sermon. Is he seriously suggesting that atheists can't enjoy their jobs, or that people with no religious faith are all depressed? But then I realize that the Preacher is using his own voyage of discovery to help people like me reflect on my life and my work.

Mark Greene writes:

> The 24 hour society. Work until 10pm, microwave meal from M&S, shop for a mortgage on the internet at midnight, check your emails at 2am. Relationships? There may be a free slot between 2 and 5.15am.[16]

Is work fulfilment found in this kind of mad-dash world where the higher you climb the faster things happen?

Vince Foster was a member of the Bill Clinton White House and a long-standing friend of the president. His suicide in 1993 prompted much speculation, although the official verdict declared that he had been suffering from clinical depression for some time. Not long before his death, he spoke to the graduating class at Arkansas University School of Law:

> A word about family. You have amply demonstrated that you are achievers willing to work hard, long hours and set aside your personal lives. But it reminds me of an observation that no one was heard to say on a deathbed, 'I wish I'd spent more time at the office'. Balance wisely your professional life and your family life. If you are fortunate enough to have children, your parents will warn you that your children will grow up and be gone before you know it. I can testify that this is true. God only allows us so many opportunities with our children to read a story, go fishing, play catch and say our prayers together. Try not to miss one of them. The office can wait. It will still be there after your children are gone.[17]

> **The office can wait. It will still be there after your children are gone.**

Work with God

I can remember our first colour television. (Come to think of it, I can remember our first black-and-white television!) The experience of watching the TV was totally transformed because the colour made things look like real life.

I have that sense when the writer of Ecclesiastes explains how work with a God-dimension gave colour to his black-and-white world. He picks out three good reasons.

1. Work with God can be satisfying

> People can do nothing better than to eat and drink and find satisfaction in their work.[18]

The desire to find fulfilment in work is not a bad thing – in fact, it can be described as a God-thing. As we have already seen in chapter 1, God the Creator stood back and took satisfaction from his work, and as those made in his image we can seek fulfilment in our tasks. Feeling that sense of satisfaction is part of what it means to be human.

2. Work should be seen as a gift from God

The phrase quoted above ends with this sentence:

> This too, I see, is from the hand of God, for without him, who can eat or find enjoyment?[19]

This raises the question of whether we have ever looked at work as a gift from God.

Luciano Pavarotti, the Italian tenor, brought opera to a wider audience largely through his rendition of Puccini's *Nessun Dorma*, which became the theme of the 1990 World Cup Final. The man with the golden voice inspired millions to listen to classical music for the first time. In a television interview he offered a simple yet heartfelt explanation of his success: 'God kissed my vocal chords.' That, I think, is what it means to see work as a gift from God.

3. Work can develop us as people

As a child I can remember those fateful words, 'You'll grow into them', as I put on a pair of hand-me-down trousers two sizes too big. 'Why can't I just have things that fit me now?' was my constant question.

The Preacher sees work as a tool that God uses to help us grow into some valuable things:

> To the one who pleases him, God gives wisdom, knowledge and happiness . . . [20]

Wisdom is what we need for skilful living, knowledge develops our understanding of life and happiness is something we all desire. These three gifts are – according to this writer – gifts that God can give through the experience of working life. In the right environment, work can help our development as people.

Key point
Work without God **can become an unfulfilling end in itself.**
Work with God **should be seen as a gift from his hand that can help us grow.**

Finding fulfilment in our work
Some years ago I was given a list of questions that I wrote down and kept. I go back to them from time to time to remind myself of my answers and check that I haven't slipped back.

> **What** am I doing?
> **Why** am I doing it?
> **How** am I doing it?
> **Who** am I doing it for?

That may come as a surprise, as you may have thought that the last person who needs to be reminded of priorities is a pastor. But in any field of work – including Christian ministry – it is possible to lose focus, and once focus is lost, direction and momentum quickly leave as well.

I want to suggest some ways in which we can view our work, whatever shape it may take, which can help us towards finding a greater sense of fulfilment in what we do.

Work can be worship

I was sitting in an airport lounge in India waiting to board my flight when a large group of tourists appeared at the gate, many of them wearing bright orange t-shirts. I discovered that they were returning from a visit to an ashram, where they had spent several weeks sitting at the feet of a guru. Most were thirty-something Europeans who had used their well-earned vacation time to make a pilgrimage to an Indian holy man. The t-shirts bore a large slogan:

Work is Worship

Work is Worship

This may have been the theme of their retreat, or perhaps an often-quoted pearl from the guru's collection – but I spotted a stunningly simple explanation of some biblical theology.

Paul encourages the Christians in Rome:

> Therefore, I urge you, brothers and sisters, in view of God's mercy, to offer your bodies as living sacrifices, holy and pleasing to God – this is your spiritual act of worship.[21]

What the NIV translators have called a 'spiritual act of worship' is translated in other versions as 'reasonable service'. In contemporary Christian culture, the word 'worship' is often shorthand for singing and prayer, but it has a broader definition than that. Worship is what we offer to God, the Father, Son and Holy Spirit, out of all that we are – including our work.

The title for this chapter is more or less borrowed from Martin Luther (1483–1546), who was a key player in the Protestant Reformation of the sixteenth century. He had a famously earthy approach to preaching and many of his congregation were farm workers. He is said to have told them on more than one occasion, 'God even milks the cow through you.' He wanted those farm workers to understand that even a mundane, routine task such as milking the cow could have holy connotations.

My friend Liz was the head teacher of a secondary school and faced many demands in her busy life. She once asked me to pray about a difficult situation that involved disciplinary action against a staff member. Potentially the case could wreck the teacher's career, but as we talked and prayed, I realized that here was a disciple of Christ working hard to make even a difficult job worship. Liz wanted to do the right thing – to the glory of God.

Satisfaction is a God-given feeling

Chris works with young offenders who have had their first brush with the law. His job is to act as a mentor and friend and hopefully steer his clients away from a life of crime. When you get involved in people's lives, it is complex and messy. Many of these teenagers have addiction problems and family breakdowns that add to the mix.

I asked Chris how he finds satisfaction in his job when his daily round consists of people failing to turn up in court or going AWOL. He gave me a list of little achievements that go to make up a good week in his life. Here is a man whose sense of worth is not seen in a big bonus scheme, but in progress in people's lives that is measured in centimetres.

Talking with Chris taught me that we need measures of fulfilment, especially when we are involved in work where encouragements are hard to find.

Work helps the world go round

Pete manages a large staff in a manufacturing company. He knows the decisions he makes can affect the livelihoods of many people. He works hard to keep the company going in what is a tough and competitive marketplace. Every day, on his drive to work, he commits his day to God in prayer, asking for wisdom to make good decisions and grace to deal with difficult people.

When asked about job satisfaction, he says his company's progress makes him feel good, especially when he knows he has played a part in its growth in recent years. He also points to the fact that he is helping his local community by keeping people in work and putting money into the local economy.

Pete has grasped that, when we work, we help the world work. And we don't have to be top executives – just ordinary people doing the ordinary things.

When we work, we act as Christ's agents in the world

Lucy works in a playgroup four mornings a week. She became involved when she was expecting her first child and now, eleven years on, she is the director of a playgroup that serves families in her community. Many are single-parent families and Lucy finds that, in addition to caring for the pre-school children, she becomes involved in their parents' problems as well.

It is not a church-based playgroup, but Lucy is relaxed and open about her faith. Through her friendship and support, some of the families have started to attend church and she has been used to bring practical help when some have needed it most.

Ask Lucy about job satisfaction and she will tell you it is found in helping people. She gets up every morning and goes to work as a special agent, for Jesus' sake.

I have suggested four ways in which we can look for satisfaction in our work. You may have others you can add to the list. The important thing is to have a list.

Key point
Finding fulfilment in our work includes:
seeing that work can be worship;
recognizing that job satisfaction is a God-given feeling;
understanding that work makes the world go round;
realizing that through our work we can act as Christ's
agents in the world.

A fisherman stood on a quayside smoking his pipe at the end of a lovely summer's day. The sun was beginning to sink in the west as he leaned silently against the harbour wall and drank in the sight.

A businessman on holiday struck up a conversation. 'Not fishing today?' he asked.

'Not this evening,' replied the fisherman. 'I've been out fishing this morning and caught all I need.'

The entrepreneur asked, 'Well, why don't you go out and catch some more?'

The fisherman replied, 'Why?'

The businessman said, 'So you can buy a bigger boat.'

The fisherman asked, 'Well, what for?'

'So you can catch more fish and you can develop your company. You can buy a fleet of boats and hire a crowd of guys.'

The fisherman asked, 'What for?'

The entrepreneur replied, 'So you can relax and enjoy life and watch the world go by.'

'So what do you think I'm doing at the moment?' asked the fisherman.

A verse we considered earlier in this chapter reminded us that godliness with contentment is great gain. That is a truth worth weighing, as you lean against the harbour wall.

For further thought . . .

1. Look at Deuteronomy 8:17–18 and 1 Timothy 6:6–10. Then reflect on this statement: 'Like many other scriptures, these two passages need to be held in balance as they teach parallel truths. The ability to create wealth is God-given, but beware of loving money so much that it destroys you.' What do you think of this statement? How does it affect the way you view your finances?

2. Compare the thoughts of the writer of Ecclesiastes about the world of work – with and without God – with your own views.

3. What gives you a sense of fulfilment in your work?

9. WHERE DO I FIT IN?

A man waited patiently to speak to me at the end of a meeting. When eventually we spoke, he produced a black-and-white photo and asked, 'Do you recognize anyone in this picture?'

It was a photograph of a school choir in full flow, and slap bang in the middle of the group was a twelve-year-old boy with a pudding-basin haircut and sporting an atrocious pair of National Health glasses.

It was me.

To make matters worse, the photographer had managed to capture a moment when I looked as if I was singing my head off whilst the fifty or so kids around me seemed much more refined in the vocal endeavours. I looked as if I was hyperactive with a capital 'H'.

My friend gave me the photograph to take home and it caused much amusement in my family. But, as they say, every picture tells a story. Later, when the laughter had died down, my wife asked me if I could remember the photograph being taken. A myriad of memories came flooding back.

The school I attended had an excellent choir and a first-class music teacher. We had won a place in the final of a national competition and had gone to London to perform. The photo I held in my hand had appeared in the local newspaper, *The Surrey Comet*, alongside a piece reporting our success. I told my wife I looked stupid in the picture and she came back with a typical response for her, full of wise insight. 'No,' she said, 'you don't look stupid. Just bursting with enthusiasm.'

I thought a lot about that photograph and what it represented. It was probably my first conscious experience of being part of a team that did something really well. The look on my twelve-year-old face said it all – I was loving what I was doing and giving the best that I could. I was singing my head off and enjoying every minute of the experience.

I found my embarrassment making way for another feeling: a longing to find that look captured in the photograph in everything I do – a longing to feel fulfilled because I know I am doing what I am good at, doing it to the very best of my ability and working alongside others who share the vision.

This chapter is about finding that good fit and – in particular – it raises the question of spiritual gifts and whether they have any bearing on our daily work.

Faith and work belong together, and that is true not just for Christians. People from other world faiths believe it too. In Judaism, work is laid aside on the Sabbath, not because work is bad, but because there is a God-ordained rhythm of life where there is time to work and time for rest. A strict fast is observed from sunrise to sunset during the annual Muslim feast of Ramadan, yet for most followers the working day continues unabated. The Hindu religion links faith and work very closely. The management of Nepal Airlines certainly practise that philosophy: one of their planes was suffering regular technical breakdowns costing the company thousands of pounds in lost business – so they sacrificed two goats to appease a Hindu god.[1]

Faith and work belong together.

In a Christian understanding of spiritual gifts, God gives special skills to all his children, to help in building up the church, the body of Christ. But do they have any place in our lives beyond the local congregation?

I believe they do, but our limited world view can inhibit their use. In this chapter we are going to consider five questions:

- What are spiritual gifts?
- Where do they come from?
- How do they operate?
- How can I discover my spiritual gift(s)?
- How do spiritual gifts fit into my work life?

What are spiritual gifts?

The Bible passage that is most often referred to on this topic is 1 Corinthians 12. There Paul, the Christian leader, makes this statement:

There are different kinds of gifts, but the same Spirit.[2]

Paul uses the word *charismaton* – translated 'gifts' in our English Bibles. The words 'charisma' and 'charismatic' have their origins here. When we use them, we are referring to a person being extremely gifted and dynamic. The Greek word *charisma* basically means a gift. It is not used very much at all in general Greek writings, which highlights its use in the New Testament. Its Christian usage conveys the idea of a gift that is free and undeserved, and some use the expression 'grace-gift' to convey the true meaning of *charisma*.

Every Christian has at least one spiritual gift.

There are several New Testament passages where various gifts are listed.[3] If we add them together, some twenty gifts are mentioned and it has been suggested that the list is not exhaustive. In other words, there could be quite a few more that can be identified. One popular writer has developed a skills inventory and questionnaire, which helps to pinpoint which of twenty-eight gifts you have been given.[4]

What seems clear is that every Christian has at least one

spiritual gift,[5] possibly more, and (put simply) they are given to equip Christ's followers to do his work in the world.

Based on my reading of the New Testament and my observations as a pastor, it is my belief that spiritual gifts are not just confined to so-called Christian activities. Spiritual gifts have a role in the workplace too.

Where do spiritual gifts come from?

The Bible is clear that these grace-gifts come from God himself. According to Paul, the whole of the Trinity is involved in giving them:

> There are different kinds of gifts, but the same Spirit. There are different kinds of service, but the same Lord. There are different kinds of working, but the same God works all of them in everyone.[6]

These gifts are freely available to the people of God, but we can't predetermine which ones we end up with. As we have seen, the gifts of the Spirit are given in order that we may serve the Lord effectively, just as the fruit of the Spirit is grown in lives that are lived in obedience to him.[7]

The fruit of the Spirit is all about the character of Christ being formed in us – that we might be like Jesus. The gifts of the Spirit are about the work of Christ being accomplished through us – that we may act like Jesus.

There seem to be two ways in which these gifts are imparted. Sometimes the Lord will give what isn't there, but on most occasions he will touch what is already there.

Giving what isn't there implies a transformation in a person's life. A gift comes from outside an individual's life experience. For example, someone with no desire to pray suddenly finds him- or herself with a deep compassion and ability to bring people's need to God in prayer. Another person who by nature is shy and retiring finds a new confidence and takes on a leadership and teaching role in a youth group.

Touching what is already there refers to people who have a natural talent, perhaps in organization, or in music or hospitality. As they offer that ability back to God, he takes and touches it in a way that takes the gift further than an individual can take it alone.

As a leader and pastor in a local church, I have noticed how we can too easily jump to hasty conclusions. We appoint people to various roles on the basis of their natural gifting, without stopping to consider whether the gift has been given back to God and is being used well. So to appoint Frank as treasurer simply because he is an accountant is not a wise move. Of course it is sensible to appoint someone with the necessary skills, but someone handling church finances needs more than the ability to keep accurate records. In my experience, a mature faith, a generous heart and the ability to think strategically in kingdom terms are three essentials for this kind of ministry.

Key point
- **Spiritual gifts come from God.**
- **Every Christian has at least one.**
- **They are given so that we can serve effectively.**

How do spiritual gifts operate?

Spiritual gifts operate as we lead our daily lives as normal, but with a conscious openness to God directing our day. Let me illustrate. I went to visit an elderly member of our church who was caring for his wife, who suffered from senile dementia. His day had started badly because his wife had not co-operated while he tried to wash and dress her. He was temporarily overwhelmed with a feeling of total despair: things would never get any better.

Then, at 8.00 a.m., his phone rang. Joy was on her way to work and felt prompted to call. A five-minute conversation, some strengthening words, a short prayer and a promise to call round later was all it took. George sat with me and shared his miracle of the day. The interesting thing is that Joy had a habit of doing this kind of thing. In fact, it was less of a habit, and more of a gift. She was an encourager and shepherd who regularly practised acts of mercy – and those were three spiritual gifts she used that Tuesday morning before she even arrived at the office.

Three words sum up the way in which spiritual gifts can operate in our daily lives: openness, opportunity and obedience.

Openness is about our willingness to let God have all we are, including our working time. It took Joy some time to understand that what she saw as a friendly word of encouragement was more than that. She began to see that God had given her spiritual gifts and wanted her to use them. She began to live in faith and openness for things to happen.

Opportunity means that we listen for God's voice and look for ways in which we can use the gifts he has entrusted to us. It involves not simply committing each day to the Lord in prayer, but also seeking to maintain a spiritual sensitivity as we meet people.

Obedience involves doing what he tells us to do when those opportunities come along.

We have already mentioned the problems caused by a compartmentalized view of life. If we hold the view that spiritual gifts can operate only when we are in church, we seek to put limits on what God can and can't do. If God has chosen to entrust a gift to you, then it is relevant in every part of your life. That doesn't mean, however, that we don't need to exercise discernment in how those gifts are used.

Key point
Spiritual gifts operate where there is:
- **openness – I am willing for my gift to be used;**
- **opportunity – I am looking for ways in which my gift can be used;**
- **obedience – I am ready for my gift to be used.**

How can I discover my spiritual gift(s)?

If you use an internet search engine, you will discover various online questionnaires designed to help you answer this question. But the best place to discover what God has for us is within the local community of the church. If we are committed to a local family of Christ's followers, then that is the place to begin to explore our calling and gifting.

There are three parallel lines of enquiry.

- Ask God.
- Ask others.
- Ask yourself.

Asking God may seem obvious, but prayer and study of what the Bible has to say about spiritual gifts have to be our starting points. We are told that we are to 'eagerly desire' spiritual gifts,[8] so it is an exercise that has heaven's backing.

Asking others underlines the importance of the wisdom of people who know us best. People in our homegroup, leaders of the congregation, or friends we spend time with are some of the sources we can approach. We are not expecting them to get our guidance for us, but rather to help us discern the guidance we seek for ourselves.

Asking yourself involves addressing some important questions, such as 'What am I good at?' or 'What do I like doing best?' or 'What do I do well at?' or 'Where are those moments when I feel fulfilled and sense God's pleasure?'

Following those three parallel lines of enquiry will help things take shape in our minds. The next step is to start using your gift and see what happens. If the gift is hospitality, then start to invite people for meals in your home; if it is the gift of encouragement, then start to make a list of those in need of some; if your gift happens to be administration, begin to look around for someone who is struggling to cope and needs a good organizer.

If I could inject one word of caution here, it would be to underline the difference between aspiration and achievement. From conversations with other church leaders, I have discovered this to be a sensitive and relevant issue. Sometimes there are individuals who long to be good at something and convince themselves that they have the gifting required, while to others it is blatantly obvious that they don't have it. For some strange reason, this often centres on music. Someone thinks she has a great singing voice, but anyone listening knows it is better used in the shower rather than in congregational worship. Another believes he is the new Graham Kendrick and sees no problem with lyrics that are predictable (of the 'loss, dross and cross' variety) and tunes that sound like nursery rhymes.

I confess to feeling worried at times when, as a church, we are not more honest with people, especially when they feel increasingly offended as their constant offers of help are politely declined. I have learned the hard way that, when such situations occur, honesty really is the best policy. I once asked a golfing teacher if he encountered pupils he knew would never make golfers. He smiled and replied, 'I learned long ago that I can't put in what God left out.'

Gifting, you see, is essential.

Key point
The best way of discovering my spiritual gift(s) is within the Christian family where I can
- **ask God;**
- **ask others;**
- **ask myself.**

How do spiritual gifts fit into my work life?

If you have a holistic view of life – which is what I believe the New Testament teaches – then life cannot be put into compartments. If we have been gifted with a pastoral heart, then that is not something we switch on because it's Tuesday night and housegroup is about to start. If it is a gift, then it has to work on Wednesday morning in the staff canteen. We don't put our gifts on the shelf like a Bible and pull them down when a meeting is about to begin.

I am not suggesting an unreal spirituality that thinks naivety and faith are the same thing. We need, in the words of Jesus, to be 'as shrewd as snakes and as innocent as doves'[9] – not to act as daft as brushes. So laying hands on the photocopier and making prophetic pronouncements about the tea rota are best left within the pages of an Adrian Plass book.

Let me take two biblical examples, followed by three real-life stories of how God's good gifts can operate wherever his people are found.

Nehemiah is an excellent example of the spiritual gift of faith. Read his book and you will see what I mean. He prayed, planned, organized and built a wall that had lain in ruins for years in just fifty-two days. To achieve this he needed to inspire and mobilize people and exercise some spiritual muscle and political acumen.

Whenever I read the book named after him, I am humbled and challenged by this man's range of abilities. He showed the kind of talent that launches entrepreneurial projects which make millions by taking hold of something that they said couldn't be done. His skill mix was quite extraordinary and his capacity to inspire others facing a stack of obstacles was miraculous. And 'miraculous' is the right word to use, because as we read his journal he continually acknowledges that what happened was down to God working through him.

Daniel is the second example and he amply displays how the spiritual gift of wisdom came to the fore during a hard day at the office. He interpreted Nebuchadnezzar's dream by relying on his God-given gifting.[10]

Here are three contemporary accounts of people who take their spiritual gifts to work on the bus.

> God had placed her in the post and he had a purpose for her to fulfil.

Sheila works in a busy city-centre hospital, where she is a nursing sister in the operating theatres. She is one of three senior staff and her two colleagues are both men. The majority of the rest of the staff who make up the team are women and many personnel issues are picked up by Sheila, often to do with health and family.

Sheila realized very early on that she was in her job for a purpose. At the time she was appointed she had been reading the book of Esther and a verse in that remarkable story had stood out for her. It contained the words 'for such a time as this'.[11] As Sheila thought about her job, she realized that God had placed her in the post and he had a purpose for her to fulfil.

She has a number of spiritual gifts that are apparent to anyone who spends time with her. She has a heart for people, which she sees as God-given, she encourages and has wisdom and a great ability to discern things. So it was no surprise to me, as her pastor, that people spoke of her special skills at work. We valued her gifts in the church – but I am so glad she didn't leave them there. They are too special.

Tom is a bricklayer, and a good one. He has worked in the building trade since he left school. He became a Christian not long after his apprenticeship ended and makes no secret about his faith. He is busy in his local church and often puts his building skills to good use. Last summer he was part of a team that spent two weeks in Zambia helping to build a small school. Tom has a special gifting in prayer and he uses it in the workplace. He prays for the men and women he works with and he does it regularly and specifically. Most don't know about his prayer ministry, because Tom doesn't think they need to know. But he has a sense that part of his role as a Christian at work is to pray for people and their needs. So he quietly gets on with what he sees as a calling from God: to be a pray-er on the building site.

There have been occasions, however, when he has talked to some of his mates about his faith. And when there has been a bereavement, a marriage break-up, or a sudden illness, he gets alongside the person concerned and says something along the lines of 'I'll pray for you'. Ask Tom if he gets his leg pulled, and he will tell you that there is some good-natured banter and occasional cynicism. But he will also tell you about some of his mates who will sidle up when no-one is listening and ask him to pray for a sick child or elderly parent. Tom could leave his praying to church and in-house requests. But he sees his gift as too special to be limited to a few hours a week.

Dave is a lawyer and we have been friends for thirty years. Every now and then over the years, he has called me and suggested a men's night in a pub or bowling alley. The venues vary, but the programme has hardly changed: some food, drink and conversation followed by an opportunity for me to share the good news about Jesus with a bunch of guys who wouldn't be seen dead in a church, no matter how 'seeker sensitive' it was.

Dave has the gift of faith sharing (evangelism, if you want to be technical) and he looks for ways to use his gift every day of the week. I have lost count of the friends he has introduced me to, all with different stories to tell of how Dave has been the main tourist guide on their journey of faith.

> **You all know the most important thing in my life is my Christian faith.**

My last outing with Dave was to a wine bar just off London's Piccadilly Circus. He invited six London-based clients to lunch in a private room. His invitation had been totally up front: good food and conversation about things that matter. I took along a friend who is a Member of Parliament, because I wanted him to share his own remarkable story of finding faith when he wasn't even looking for it.

Dave began with an introduction that ran like this: 'We are good friends and spend time talking about all kinds of things – business, family, sport and politics. But, as you all know, the most important thing in my life is my Christian faith. I've invited Ian to talk to us today about how we can find that faith for ourselves and how knowing Christ makes life make sense . . . '

It won't surprise you to know that many people – clients, colleagues, friends and neighbours – have come to faith through Dave using his gift. Through friendship and conversation he has been used to help many people. I thank God that he didn't leave his gift for Sundays. It is much too special for that.

The risk in sharing stories like those of Sheila, Tom and Dave is that some of us react by thinking, 'I could never do that!' But that is to miss the point. It is about exercising the gift(s) God has given you in the place he has put you.

If the Lord Jesus has given you a spiritual gift – or more than one – it is to be used to build up the church, his body. But don't leave his gifts for the Christian community alone. They are too special.

Youth groups often come up with intriguing names or titles. The best I ever heard was simply called 'No Limits'. They wanted it to convey a sense of welcome to newcomers – there were no limits to who could attend. But the young people who made up the group also wanted to find a way of summing up what they understood about being followers of Christ.

'No Limits' says it all.

For further thought . . .

1. Can you identify a gift (or gifts) God has given to you?

2. Review what is said about Sheila, Tom and Dave – plus Nehemiah and Daniel. What do their stories say to you about using your gifts beyond the four walls of the church?

3. How can we better help people in our church to identify what God has gifted them to do?

POSTSCRIPT: NOTES FROM A PASTOR'S CASEBOOK

Few would deny that there have been massive and important changes in Western society in the past fifty years – and both home and the workplace have been radically affected.

This is illustrated by the following extract from an article in a best-selling magazine in the 1950s. The topic of the article was how a woman should prepare for her husband's return from work.

Take 15 minutes to rest so you'll be refreshed when he arrives. Touch up your make-up, put a ribbon in your hair and be fresh looking.

Be a little gay and a little more interesting for him. His boring day may need a lift and one of your duties is to provide it.

- At the time of his arrival, eliminate all noise of the washer, dryer or vacuum. Try to encourage the children to be quiet.
- Listen to him. You may have a dozen important things to tell him, but the moment of his arrival is not the time. Let him talk first – remember, his topics of conversation are more important than yours.
- Make the evening his. Never complain if he comes home late or goes out to dinner, or other places of entertainment without you. Instead try to understand his world of strain and pressure.
- Arrange his cushion and offer to take off his shoes. Speak in a low, soothing and pleasant voice.

- Don't ask him questions about his actions. Remember, he is the master of the house and as such will always exercise his will with fairness and truthfulness. You have no right to question him.[1]

My wife read that extract to me with a level of incredulity that would probably have qualified for the *Guinness Book of Records*. Leave aside the blatant sexism, if you can, and notice the assumption that the man is the breadwinner and the wife stays at home. But life as we once knew it has changed. Standing in our kitchen a few minutes ago, we did a swift calculation and identified six couples in our circle of contacts where the wife has the career and the husband runs the home full-time. (We intend to check with each couple if the above instructions on how to welcome your spouse work for them!)

There is a hymn that contains the verse:

Through all the changing scenes of life,
In trouble and in joy,
The praises of my God shall still
My heart and tongue employ.[2]

Whatever changes take place in the greater world or in our smaller world, those who choose to follow Christ can rest easy that he is the constant one. Whatever else may change, Jesus doesn't.[3]

Fashions come and go, cultures undergo massive shift and history records changes that would once have been considered impossible. Many of those changes we would accept as being for the greater good. When the Bible speaks of Jesus as Lord, it includes his authority over the movement of history. One well-known hymn describes him as 'the potentate of time'.[4]

We can confidently face life in the light of the truth that Jesus is the unique Time Lord, and, whatever changes in the world around us, he is in ultimate control.

Writing this book has made me think carefully about some of those I have met during my Christian journey. Having been involved in Christian ministry for over three decades, I have sat and listened, talked and prayed with many people who have shared deeply about their lives and jobs. In this final chapter I want to highlight briefly some common struggles faced in the workplace, and suggest some practical responses.

Integrating two worlds

John Beckett has sold a lot of books – for an engineer. His first book, *Loving Monday: Succeeding in Business without Selling Your Soul*,[5] has become a worldwide best-seller and tells how he guided his family business to worldwide leadership in the manufacture and sale of components for residential and commercial heating.

That book was followed up with a second, *Mastering Monday: Experiencing God's Kingdom in the Workplace*.[6] In this book, he has a chapter entitled 'Integrating Two Worlds', which frankly describes his spiritual journey. He tells of a time when he began to realize that God had put him in business for a bigger purpose than making lots of money. He writes:

> [I made] a clear commitment to the Lord in response: I would do all I could to bring my faith to work. I wouldn't be one person on Sunday and another on Monday. I would avoid 'business as usual', with its cut corners and compromise. I would try to lead our company in ways that would honour and please him.

Thus began my journey to integrate two worlds. To my surprise, I found that my growing faith was often relevant to work issues – but the reverse was also true. Workplace issues challenged and strengthened my faith, occasionally more than I'd anticipated.[7]

John Beckett's story has been repeated many times by people of all backgrounds who reach the point of spiritual dissatisfaction at being two-world disciples. In his writings he details how the shift from two worlds to one worked for him. This integration process affected the values, vision and principles of his whole business.[8]

The shift from two-world to one-world vision begins with a commitment and an invitation. The *commitment* is to see change happen and the *invitation* is for Christ to fill our workspace. We can become too worried about the details of how specific problems will be handled. But they will fall into place if the commitment and the invitation are genuine.

Workaholics Anonymous

Some are eaten up by their work to such an extent that we have coined a word to describe them: workaholics. It plays on the idea that in the same way we can become addicted to substances like alcohol, we can become addicted to work.

Thankfully, people who see their lives wrecked by drink or drugs can find help if they really want it. Doctors, counsellors, programmes, clinics and support groups exist. But where do you go if you're addicted to your job?

Let's be clear: there is a difference between being busy, carrying heavy responsibility, working long hours and being a work addict. I know plenty of hard workers who are anything but workaholics. The difference is most starkly seen and understood when the job is unmasked as a substitute for something else. For example, long hours at work can mean avoiding dealing with relationships at home. The desire to put in more hours than anyone else can be a substitute for a parent's missing 'well done'. Workaholism is when work becomes an excuse for not engaging in real life.

The adage puts it well: we are meant to work to live, not live to work.

I have seen workaholism in a number of friends, some of whom have ruined their health and marriages *en route*.

The work of Alcoholics Anonymous is truly amazing and one of the great strengths of the movement is the strong emphasis on mutual support. The transparent vulnerability of the group is balanced by the sense that you do not fight the battle alone. I think there is a valuable pastoral model here that would help many of us in our personal struggles in life. Anyone who is seriously worried about their attitude to work needs to share it. That may be with a work colleague, or even a doctor or pastor.

Workaholism is when work becomes an excuse for not engaging in real life.

A second step forward for a recovering workaholic is to create accountable friendships. Find another Christian with whom you can pray and talk freely about the pressures you face. The fifteenth-century mystic St Teresa of Avila wrote:

When you start to pray, get yourself some company.[9]

That is wonderfully practical advice. Seek someone with whom you can pray about your world of work. As I write these words, I can look back over thirty or so years and thank

God for a list of people who have been prayer partners with me in my world of work. Paul, David and Tony, Mike, Nathan and Nigel are men who have walked with me as I have struggled with issues of work and life. People like them are out there and eager to find someone like you. Start by praying and looking around.[10]

'I'm a nobody'

There are people who feel no sense of worth in who they are or what they do.

Take Kim as an example. In her mid-forties and single, she is the primary carer for her father, who suffers from Alzheimer's. Her happiest time at work was working in a large department store, where her friendly personality made her an ideal sales assistant. Customers went out of their way to comment on her abilities and within a few years she was in a management role with special responsibility for the induction of new staff. Life changed dramatically when Kim's mum underwent major surgery and needed full-time post-operative care.

At first Kim's company were happy to offer extended compassionate leave, but eventually she and they could see that she would be unable to return to work for many months. Reluctantly they let her go, both sides hoping that when Kim's mum eventually died she would be able to return to work. Tragically, when her mum did die, her father became so ill and confused that he also needed full-time care and Kim's role of nurse switched from one parent to the other.

If you and I were to sit and share a coffee with Kim, it would not be long into the conversation before we talked about her home circumstances and detected the note of sadness as she talked about her role as a long-term carer. There would be no trace of bitterness in her voice, because she is convinced that what she has done to serve her mother and is now doing to serve her father are her proper responsibilities as an only daughter. But she deeply mourns the loss of a job, some good friends, a regular payslip – and, most of all, that sense of being a somebody.

There is probably someone like Kim in your church. They may be caring for small children rather than elderly relatives, but the issue remains the same. They can't produce a job title or point to an annual pay review, but they work as hard as – if not harder than –those of us in such privileged positions.

How can Kim find value in her everyday work? There are no quick-fix answers and, in my experience, people like Kim are the ones who need maximum support from a local church. Sadly they are often overlooked, as somehow carers don't rank as high in our pastoral care as those whose needs seem much more apparent.

People who offer care – whether for elderly relatives or small children – need top-level support. The shape of that support will vary, but at base level it means a small group who can share the load. That may mean a listening ear, the practical response of offering to babysit (or grandad-sit), cooking a meal or praying hard when the pressure grows. Carers need caring for too.

Carers need caring for too.

Kim is part of a caring church where such support exists, but she will tell you that there came a point two years ago when she saw her vicar and explained that she needed something more. He was wise enough to read this as a cry for help rather than a criticism, and a small pastoral support group included Kim on their list of people to look out for. Someone meets Kim every few weeks to look at practical ways she can receive help. She looks forward to those times as regular opportunities to offload the burden of responsibility she carries day after day.

The issue of self-worth goes much deeper and Kim is having to work on gaining a clearer understanding of who she is in Christ. Recently her homegroup have been studying Paul's letter to the Philippians. Kim was really helped by one passage in which Paul wrote about discovering the secret of contentment.[11] Since that time she has been doing a lot of thinking and praying around that idea, in the hope that one day she will find the secret for herself.

Promotion – or not?

What do you do when a plum promotion is offered – bigger salary, better car, loads more challenges, plus a move to a brand-new area of the country?

Well, what *do* you do?

That is a good question to ask, because the answer will reveal how involved God is in our world of work. The wise words of Proverbs caution us:

> Trust in the LORD with all your heart
>   and lean not on your own understanding;
> in all your ways acknowledge him,
>   and he will make your paths straight.[12]

If we take these words seriously, then it is not the company you work for that should decide where you live and what you do. Acknowledging God means taking our plans and our opportunities to him – and listening hard for his directions. I have lost count of the times when I have realized to my shame that I am leaning on my own understanding instead of looking for God's way.

I can vividly remember Mark coming to see me one evening after work. He and his wife, Yvonne, were members of our church and busily involved in running a student ministry. I had conducted their wedding and the two had become good friends of our family.

Mark had been approached out of the blue to take on a new job – but it would mean moving abroad. There were enormous implications all round. We talked and prayed and agreed to give matters a couple of weeks then meet again. They were not expecting me to get their guidance, but as I was their pastor they wanted me to be on the sidelines supporting them as they prayed and weighed the options.

When we met again, Mark was visibly moved as he recounted how the two of them, in various ways, had reached the conclusion that this was an opportunity the Lord was opening for them. My prayers from the sidelines had led me to the same place. We both wept, as we knew that this meant they would leave a safe spiritual home where they had identity, ministry and some special friends. I felt the tug of love in giving away one of our best couples at the very time when we were expanding the church's work with students. But, when the time came to say farewell, we could look each other in the eyes and say, 'The Lord is in this!'

About six weeks ago, I sat with Mark and Yvonne and listened as they recounted just a few of the many good things God had accomplished through their move of faith. Job, family, church, friendships – all had flourished, in spite of some inevitable setbacks and disappointments. My mind went back to a tearful pastoral appointment many years before and my heart was lifted in praise for a pair of disciples who took their faith seriously enough to consult Jesus in the job stakes.

Disabled by disappointment

Many know the name Lewis Hamilton, but few know Wesley Graves, even though at one stage the two seemed to share a common destiny.

Lewis Hamilton has become a world-famous Formula One driver and a hot contender for a World Championship title, while Wesley is unemployed and spends much of his time sitting at home. The two of them were spotted as boys who showed a precocious talent for speed in the world of go-karting. The Formula One manufacturing team McLaren signed them both up. Lewis was thirteen and Wesley just twelve years of age. After just one year the decision was made to retain Lewis and drop Wesley. I read a depressing interview with Wesley a few days ago.[13]

It is obvious that neither he nor his family have recovered from the sense of rejection and disappointment. His parents have lost their business and their home through heavy spending in an attempt to restart their son's career. He admits he can't watch Grand Prix racing on television because it hurts too much. It is estimated that Lewis could become the wealthiest British sports star of all time, but Wesley's prospects appear much bleaker.

I sense that – at least for now – Wesley has become disabled by disappointment and I have met many in similar circumstances. Their story may not be quite as dramatic, but it has left the same residue of pain.

It can stem from redundancy, from being by-passed for promotion, from an unfair dismissal, or from a job in which everything simply went wrong. What is left behind is someone who is hurt, angry and desperately disappointed.

A colleague on the staff of a church where we were both pastors called on a family in the community. There was a relatively minor issue to do with their teenage son who was a member of the youth group. What started as a low-temperature conversation quickly switched to full heat as the father erupted in uncontrolled anger. It looked as if this pastoral visit was about to end in a fist-fight. Anxious to avoid giving a whole new meaning to spiritual warfare, my colleague retreated both shaken and stirred.

We needed to follow things up and in the process a sad story emerged. The father had held a relatively prestigious job for a number of years, but as a result of a takeover his services were surplus to requirements. These were days when employment law was much looser and he was paid off with a pittance, with no hope of any justice being brought to his case.

We discovered that he had never worked again, but lived on the poison of his bitterness. Anything and anyone who represented authority became the target for venom: the local council extending the no-parking zone, the teacher who sent a child home with an unfavourable report, the greengrocer who put up prices, a Baptist minister who popped round to talk over the minor skirmishes of an adolescent. It is a pastoral fact observable every day of the week – hurt people, hurt people.

As I have watched people struggle with such hurts, I have come to understand that there is a choice we face when disappointment strikes. The choice is whether we allow it to control us or choose to channel it. If it controls us, we face a long road of bitter memories and unforgiveness. If we make the choice to channel it, there is every possibility that we can grow into better people, by God's grace.

I recognize that this may take time and often skilled counselling. But the choice is the key.

Ministries-R-Us

I have had many conversations with people exploring the possibility that God may be calling them into some form of full-time ministry. I have one piece of advice that I share at the start: do everything you can to steer well clear of it.

Christian ministry is not about career choice. It begins with the call of God on a person's life that is probably best summed up by the prophet Amos in his reply to the professional priest who sought to silence him:

> I was neither a prophet nor a prophet's son, but I was a shepherd, and I also took care of sycamore-fig trees. But the LORD took me from tending the flock and said to me, 'Go, prophesy to my people Israel.'[14]

It was the call of God that made Amos leave his job. And that same sense of calling held him steady when the tide of public opinion threatened to knock him off his feet.

The call of God is the primary qualification for any form of Christian ministry. As the advert for a famous credit card says, 'Don't leave home without it.'

In advising people to steer well clear of Christian ministry, I am seeking to make the point that, if God is calling them, they won't be able to avoid it. By all means seek advice, examine what is involved and pray over the issue – but don't pursue it as a career choice. Most of all, don't explore the possibility because your current job is boring. It is all too easy to have a 'grass is greener' view of ministry that is totally unrealistic. Being a full-time Christian worker carries all the frustrations of any job – plus a few you haven't thought of.

It may be that where you are now is the ministry to which the Lord has called you. But if he does have something different in store, you can trust him to show you at the right time.

Growing and learning

Germaine Greer is quoted as saying, 'You are only young once, but you can be immature forever.'[15]

Educationalists have coined the phrase 'lifelong learning' to remind us that education is not something we start and then stop. It is a process, a journey, and, some would add, an adventure.

It is a good note on which to end this book, as a few days ago I read an article with the headline 'God on Monday – the Bible and Business'.[16] It was written by Dr Richard Higginson,[17] who reported on research on the topic of things prayed about in church services. Here is his league table of prayer items.

- Frequently: clergy, church workers and missionaries.
- Quite often: those in the caring professions; teachers, doctors, nurses and social workers.
- Now and again: those in positions of national leadership, or responsible for the maintenance of law and order; politicians, police and the armed forces.
- Almost never: those involved in the commercial world, e.g. salespeople, accountants and engineers.

Reading this list, I realized (to my shame) that I am responsible for planning and leading public worship and this is an honest summary of my own prayer topics. And that is something that needs to change.

I am learning yet another important lesson about how a life of faith and the world of work can be better integrated.

Some researchers into lifelong learning conducted a survey of people of different ages to discover what new lessons were being picked up along the way. My favourite response came from a 93-year-old man who said, 'I am learning that – even at my age – I still have a lot to learn.' He is not alone.

For further thought . . .

1. How do you cope with change? What have you learned about responding to it positively?

2. This chapter highlights six common struggles I have seen people face in relation to work. Can you identify any others, perhaps ones that you or Christians you know have faced?

3. The book concludes with the topic of lifelong learning. What are you learning at present?

4. What insights from this book have particularly helped you? Is there anything for you to do or think differently as a result? Talk to God about your reflections.

NOTES

Introduction
1. Romans 12:1, *The Message.*

Chapter 1: Curse or blessing?
1. Genesis 3:17–19.
2. Genesis 3:23.
3. Genesis 1:31.
4. Genesis 1:26–27 NIVI.
5. Psalm 8:4–6 NIVI.
6. Matthew 22:37–40.
7. Genesis 1:28.
8. Genesis 2:15–17.
9. Genesis 2:18.
10. 1 Corinthians 15:20–22.
11. William Barclay, *Prayers for the Christian Year* (New York: Harper, 1965).

Chapter 2: What does God do on Mondays?
1. Colossians 3:24.
2. Colossians 3:2.
3. Colossians 3:22 – 4:1.
4. Julius Caesar, in his campaigns in Gaul (between 58 and 51 BC), is reported to have shipped back to Italy nearly 1 million prisoners of war who were consigned to lives of slavery.
5. Slavery does exist in our twenty-first-century world. According to the United Nations, 20 million people are affected by bonded labour and the International Labour Organization reports that 179 million children are engaged in work that is harmful to their health and welfare. People-trafficking has become a feature of modern crime in Europe, where governments are

responding with new legislation. Many caught up in this are young women who are dragged unwillingly into the sex industry. For further information, see www.antislavery.org.

6. Colossians 3:23–24 NIVI.

7. Colossians 4:1.

8. 2 Timothy 1:12.

9. 1 Corinthians 7:17–24 NIVI (italics mine).

10. Colossians 3:23 NIVI.

11. Matthew 22:21.

12. Colossians 3:25.

13. Colossians 4:1.

14. Colossians 3:17.

Chapter 3: I hate my job!

1. Daniel 1:1.

2. Daniel 1:2.

3. G. Campbell Morgan.

4. P. T. Forsyth, *Positive Preaching and the Modern Mind* (New York: Armstrong, 1907), p. 47.

5. Proverbs 4:23.

6. Daniel 1:8–17.

7. Daniel 1:8.

8. Read the original account in Daniel 6:1ff.

9. Daniel 6:26.

10. Daniel 1:17.

11. Daniel 2:27.

12. Deuteronomy 8:17–18.

Chapter 4: 'On yer bike!'

1. For an account of Paul's visit, see Acts 17:1–9.

2. 1 Thessalonians 3:6.

3. 2 Thessalonians 3:6 NIVI.

4. 1 Thessalonians 4:11–12.

5. See Bruce W. Winter, *Seek the Welfare of the City: Christians as Benefactors and Citizens* (Carlisle: Paternoster, 1994), pp. 41–60.

6. 1 Thessalonians 3:11.
7. 1 Corinthians 9:18.
8. 2 Thessalonians 3:7–9.
9. 2 Thessalonians 3:10.
10. 2 Thessalonians 3:12.
11. 2 Thessalonians 3:14–15 NIVI.
12. See, for example, Paul's comments to Titus, who pastored congregations on the island of Crete: Titus 1:12–13.
13. Ecclesiastes 7:18 NIVI.
14. Krish Kandiah, *Twenty-Four: Integrating Faith and Real Life* (Bletchley: Authentic, 2007), p. 51.
15. 2 Thessalonians 3:13 NIVI.

Chapter 5: Like a candle in the wind

1. See Genesis 37:3, where it is referred to as a 'richly ornamented robe'. The popular musical *Joseph and the Amazing Technicolour Dreamcoat* (by Tim Rice and Andrew Lloyd-Webber) has not quite got the wardrobe correct, it would seem! David Pawson writes: 'It was more likely a coat specifically with long sleeves, rather than any kind of multicoloured garment – the major point being that Joseph was made a foreman over the others and wore attire which emphasised he did not have to do manual work. Such preference was odd since Joseph was not the oldest son, so it led to considerable resentment.' See J. David Pawson, *Unlocking the Bible Omnibus* (London: Harper Collins, 2003), p. 88.
2. See Genesis 37:12ff. for the full story.
3. See Genesis 39:2–6.
4. See 1 Samuel 2:30.
5. Les Worrall and Cary Cooper, *The Quality of Working Life, 1999 Survey of Managers' Changing Experiences*, Institute of Management, quoted in an article by Mark Greene, Director of The London Institute for Contemporary Christianity, in *Christianity Magazine*, June 2000.
6. Reported in the *Daily Mail*, 10 May 2000.

7. See the BUPA website on stress in the workplace: http://hcd2. bupa.co.uk/fact_sheets/html/stress_workplace.html

8. The full account is found in Genesis 39:6–20.

9. See Proverbs 1:7.

10. Genesis 39:10.

11. Martin Kelly, quoted in the *Baptist Times*, April 2000.

12. Genesis 39:20–23.

13. See Genesis 50:19–21 when Joseph, at the height of his power, chooses to forgive his brothers who betrayed him. His statement of faith is truly remarkable.

14. Psalm 105:18–19.

15. Compare Genesis 37:5–11 with 42:6.

16. Pawson, *Unlocking the Bible Omnibus*, p. 92.

Chapter 6: When I'm sixty-four

1. Ecclesiastes 3:1.

2. Psalm 23:6.

3. Speech to Labour Party Conference, September 1999.

4. Debra's astonishing story can be found in *The Journey – How to Achieve Against the Odds* (Shoal Projects Ltd, 2007).

5. Ecclesiastes 9:10.

6. Matthew 6:25–34.

7. Matthew 6:33.

Chapter 7: With a little help from my friends

1. For further information, visit their website www.lionhearts.org.uk.

Chapter 8: Milking cows for Jesus?

1. Deuteronomy 8:17–18.

2. 1 Timothy 6:6–10 NIVI.

3. For a readable and practical explanation of the message of Ecclesiastes, see Derek Tidball, *That's Just the Way It Is – A Realistic View of Life* (Ross-shire: Christian Focus Publications, 1998).

4. 'Preacher' is the English translation of the Hebrew word *Qoheleth* and the Greek word *Ecclesiastes*. It describes ' "an

assembler of people into the presence of God" – a function
that is carried out today by Christian pastors. Since the
word is clearly not a personal name but a reference to an
office, the contents of the book very likely have to do with
concerns that a religious leader in the community has for
the health of the people who assemble under his or her
leadership.' See Eugene H. Peterson, *Five Smooth Stones for
Pastoral Work* (Grand Rapids: Eerdmans, 1992), pp. 156–157.

5. Ecclesiastes 1:2.
6. Ecclesiastes 1:12–18.
7. Ecclesiastes 2:1–3.
8. Ecclesiastes 2:4.
9. Ecclesiastes 2:7–8a.
10. Ecclesiastes 2:8b–9.
11. Ecclesiastes 2:10–11.
12. Ecclesiastes 2:17.
13. Ecclesiastes 2:18.
14. Ecclesiastes 2:19 NIVI.
15. Ecclesiastes 2:22–23 NIVI.
16. Mark Greene, Slave New World (www.licc.org.uk).
17. Quoted in Rob Parsons, The Sixty Minute Father (London: Hodder and Stoughton, 1995).
18. Ecclesiastes 2:24 NIVI.
19. Ecclesiastes 2:24–25.
20. Ecclesiastes 2:26 NIVI.
21. Romans 12:1 NIVI.

Chapter 9: Where do I fit in?

1. Reported in *The Week*, 8 September 2007.
2. 1 Corinthians 12:4.
3. In addition to 1 Corinthians 12:12–31, the other main passages are 1 Corinthians 14:1–40; Romans 12:6–8; Ephesians 4:7–13; and 1 Peter 4:7–11.
4. C. Peter Wagner, *Discover Your Spiritual Gifts* (Ventura, California: Regal Books, 2005).

5. 'It is inconceivable to Paul that there should be any Christian without some gift of grace. At the same time, a single individual may be characterised by more than one gift of grace.' See Colin Brown (ed.), *The New International Dictionary of New Testament Theology*, vol. 2 (Exeter: Paternoster Press, 1976), p. 121.
6. 1 Corinthians 12:4–6 NIVI.
7. For a list of the fruit of the Spirit, see Galatians 5:22–25.
8. 1 Corinthians 14:1.
9. Matthew 10:16.
10. See Daniel 2:27ff. and notice how Daniel is not slow in crediting to God's gift his ability to interpret Nebuchadnezzar's dream.
11. Esther 4:14.

Postscript: Notes from a pastor's casebook

1. *Housekeeping Monthly*, 13 May 1955.
2. Words by Nahum Tate (1652–1715) and Nicholas Brady (1659–1726).
3. Hebrews 13:8.
4. 'Crown Him With Many Crowns', words by Matthew Bridges (1800–94).
5. John D. Beckett, *Loving Monday: Succeeding in Business without Selling Your Soul* (Nottingham: IVP, 1998).
6. John D. Beckett, *Mastering Monday: Experiencing God's Kingdom in the Workplace* (Nottingham: IVP, 2006).
7. Ibid., p. 22.
8. What John Beckett describes as his 'Corporate Roadmap' can be viewed at www.beckettcorp.com.
9. Quoted by Jonathan Aitken in detailing the value of prayer partnerships in his own spiritual journey of discovery. See Jonathan Aitken, *Pride and Perjury* (London: HarperCollins, 2000), p. 266.
10. Men seem to find it more difficult to form prayer partnerships, and an organization that seeks to help can be found at www.lionhearts.org.uk.

11. See Philippians 4:10–13.

12. Proverbs 3:5–6.

13. Reported in *The Week*, 11 August 2007, pp. 48–49.

14. Amos 7:14–15.

15. Quoted in the *Independent*, July 2007.

16. *Encounter with God, Bible Reading Notes*, July – September 2007 (Milton Keynes: Scripture Union), pp. 92–95.

17. Dr Richard Higginson is Lecturer in Ethics and Leadership at Ridley Hall and Director of the Ridley Hall Foundation, a long-term project concerned with relating Christian faith to the business world. He is co-editor of the quarterly journal *Faith in Business*, and the author of *Transforming Leadership* (SPCK) and *Questions for Business Life* (Spring Harvest).

RESOURCES

Books and Booklets

Anointed for Business by Ed Silvoso (Regal Books)

Crossway Bible Guides – edited by Ian Coffey and Stephen Gaukroger (Crossway)

Discover Your Spiritual Gifts by C. Peter Wagner (Regal Books)

Get a Life – Winning Choices for Working People by Paul Valler (IVP, UK)

Globalisation and the Good by Peter Heslam (SPCK)

God at Work by Ken Costa (Continuum)

God in Work by Christian Schumacher (Lion Hudson)

Life Balance A Five-session Course on Rest, Work and Play by Robert Warren and Sue Mayfield (Church House Publishing)

Love Work Live Life by David Oliver (Authentic Media)

Loving Monday by John Beckett (IVP, USA)

Mastering Monday (book and audio CD) by John Beckett (IVP, UK)

Pocket Prayers for Work compiled by Mark Greene (Church House Publishing)

Rebuilding Trust in Business: Enron and Beyond by Nick Spencer (Grove booklet)

Supporting Christians at Work by Mark Greene (Administry and LICC)

Thank God it's Monday: Ministry in the Workplace by Mark Greene (Scripture Union)

The Busy Christian's Guide to Busyness by Tim Chester (IVP, UK)

Transition – The Christian Handbook to Life After Graduation by Tim Vickers (UCCF)

Other resources

Leadership and Followership by Jill Garrett CD Talk (LICC)
Six Sigma Jack vs Iron Joe CD Talk by Curt Hopkins (LICC)
WorkTalk CD, Tape or DVD Pack by Geoff Shattock
   (worknetuk.org.uk)

Websites

www.godatwork.org.uk
www.ivpbooks.com/faithatwork
www.lionhearts.org.uk
Aims to inspire and unite Christian men towards a more
   adventurous life with God
www.licc.org.uk
www.lovingmonday.com
www.worknetuk.org

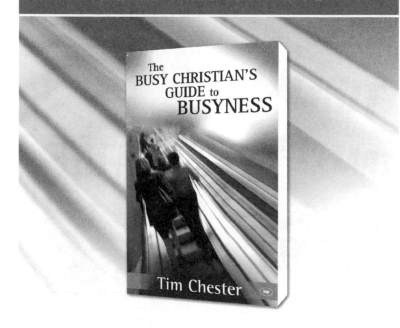

www.ivpbooks.com

For more details of books published by IVP, visit our website where you will find all the latest information, including:

Book extracts   Downloads
Author interviews   Online bookshop
Reviews   Christian bookshop finder

You can also sign up for our regular email newsletters, which are tailored to your particular interests, and tell others what you think about this book by posting a review.

We publish a wide range of books on various subjects including:

Christian living   Small-group resources
Key reference works   Topical issues
Bible commentary series   Theological studies